D1083156

THE THEOLOGY OF GRACE

IS VOLUME

23

OF THE

Twentieth Century Encyclopedia of Catholicism

UNDER SECTION

II

THE BASIC TRUTHS

IT IS ALSO THE

18TH

VOLUME IN ORDER OF PUBLICATION

Edited by HENRI DANIEL-ROPS of the Académie Française

THE THEOLOGY OF GRACE

By JEAN DAUJAT

Translated from the French by a NUN OF STANBROOK ABBEY

HAWTHORN BOOKS · PUBLISHERS · *New York*

 This book was manufactured in the United States of America and published simultaneously in Canada by McClelland & Stewart, Ltd., 25 Hollinger Road, Toronto 16. It was originally published in France under the title, *La Grâce et nous Chrétiens*. © Librairie Arthème Fayard, 1956. The Library of Congress has catalogued The Twentieth Century Encyclopedia of Catholicism under card number 58-14327. Catalogue Card No. for this volume: 59-6726.

First Edition, May, 1959

NIHIL OBSTAT

Andreas Moore, L.C.L.

Censor Deputatus

IMPRIMATUR

E. Morrogh Bernard

Vicarius Generalis

Westmonasterii, die IV FEBRUARII MCMLIX

CUM PERMISSU SUPERIORUM O.S.B.

CONTENTS

CHAPTER I

GENERAL INTRODUCTION TO GRACE

A series of books intended to expound the Christian religion as a whole must contain a volume on grace. It is a subject misunderstood by non-Catholics and hardly appreciated by Catholics, who retain of it only the vague notions remaining after their catechism lessons on a doctrine that is perhaps the most difficult in the whole course, and learnt, possibly, at the age of eleven or twelve.

Certain people after hearing a sermon or reading a pious book have an idea that by grace is meant some sort of assistance which God gives us to facilitate our own efforts or complete the merits of our good actions. But since they do not know in what such assistance consists, or know only that it is something incomprehensible, they think vaguely that it is simpler not to concern themselves with it and that, on a last analysis, the surer means of saving their souls is to count upon themselves and the merits of their good deeds. So convinced are they that they can save themselves and gain eternal life through their virtuous lives, that they fall into the Pelagian heresy, which is explained later in this book, for many Christians are Pelagians without knowing it.

Others, knowing or feeling that they are sinners, look upon grace as a pardon, or rather as a wiping out or a diminution of punishment, which God grants them rather as the Head of a state may use his right to pardon a criminal or commute the death penalty. But this kind of "grace" would serve merely to save them a punishment, without transforming them in the least, without changing them interiorly, and thus, again without knowing it, they fall into the heresy of Luther or Calvin.

Yet others, understanding literally certain metaphorical expressions used in devout works, consider grace to be a kind of religious feeling, of which one is aware within oneself, like a pleasant psychological condition, perceptible to the emotions or the conscience; this conception became widespread owing to the influence of the religious sentimentality of Jean-Jacques Rousseau, Chateaubriand and the French and, above all, the German romantic writers. Thus a person thinks he is receiving a "grace" when, in his practices of devotion, he is aware of sensible consolation, a feeling of sentimental satisfaction, some peace or some thrill or sensation of affection, some activity of his emotional make-up. On the other hand, he will think himself deprived of grace when he experiences interior aridity or dryness, when he feels nothing of the above impressions. The consequence is that those in this category fall into the Immanentist heresy of which we shall have more to say later; it is also very widespread among unbelievers, who imagine that they are lost to the faith and to Christianity because deprived of the grace which God refuses them, seeing that they feel nothing, are unaware of any religious sentiment or sensation. By the word "grace" such souls understand some manifestation of God, evident to the senses, which does not take place.

Finally, those who have received some education know that controversies about grace occurred in the seventeenth century. Some of the greatest writers of that period wrote a *Traité de la nature et de la grâce*—"Treatise on Nature and Grace"—and the controversy between the Jansenists and their opponents, followed by that on Quietism, set at stake the entire theology of grace. Nor did these controversies concern only Pascal (behind whom could be discerned Arnauld and Nicole, Saint-Cyran and de Sacy), St Francis de Sales, St Vincent de Paul, Malebranche, Leibniz, Bossuet, Fénelon and Bourdaloue, but they roused passionate feeling in the drawing-rooms and the court, in the world of letters and politics, and found an echo in the works of Corneille and Racine. Yet those who have read Pascal, Bossuet and Fénelon have not usually read St Augustine and St Thomas Aquinas, still less Jansenius and Molina, and perceive only the political and literary repercussions of controversies the basic principles of which they fail to see. For the most part, the expressions "efficacious grace" and "sufficient grace" convey nothing to them because to their minds the very notion of what grace is remains vague.

To abandon all hope of instructing our contemporaries in the doctrine of grace must be simply to abandon the attempt to instruct them concerning Christianity itself or to train them to live by it, for in the Catholic religion grace is not a subject of secondary importance, superadded by those speculative theologians who take pleasure in complicating matters, but a fundamental reality. It is the essential and the whole of the Catholic religion, so that it may be said that to speak of the latter is to speak of grace: that whenever we expound the faith we are expounding grace; that whenever we treat of any point whatsoever of Catholic doctrine we are treating of one of the aspects of grace. The Christian religion may be defined as the revelation that God loves us and, as we shall see, the effect of that love is none other than grace. We may define it also as the revelation that God is our Father, and we shall see that grace rightly consists in making of us children of God with the right to call him by that title; so that every time we say the Lord's Prayer we are talking about grace.

Again, we may define the Catholic faith as being the revelation that in God there are Three Persons and that we are taken into the "society" of those Three Persons, and we shall see that grace means that life in that society. Yet another definition is that the Christian religion is the revelation that we have been saved by Jesus Christ, which means that he gives us the grace of which he is the source. Finally, grace is defined as the life of Christ in us: the divine indwelling. Hence the Christian life is grace and grace is the Christian life. That is why the controversies over grace were of such importance in the Catholic centuries.

It is therefore a fundamental problem with which we are about to deal in this book, and the chief difficulty lies in the fact that on account of the central place which the doctrine of grace holds in the Catholic faith it is impossible to treat of the subject without touching upon every aspect of our religion and upon all the Christian mysteries with which it is bound up.

We have stated to what a degree the very word "grace" is as a sealed book for the majority of Catholics. But the word is used in several senses other than those of Catholic theology, and it is worth while to examine into its origin and different meanings in order the better to understand how it came to be introduced into the Christian vocabulary.

The word "grace" is a literal translation of the Latin *gratia*, equivalent to the Greek *charis* and derived from the Latin adjective *gratus*, meaning "pleasing". Thence is derived the sense of something granted to someone, as being pleasing to him without its being strictly his due, a gratuitous favour granted to an individual without its being an obligation, and finally a "pardon", a free remission of a penalty incurred. The word has also an important use in aesthetics, so that La Fontaine says it means "something still more than beauty", and another French writer remarks that the word suggests something that charms us because expressing or symbolizing something supremely lovable and attractive, such as trust, tenderness, etc. Thus there is a sense in which grace stands for moral qualities. On a last analysis, love is the essence of grace. What we admire in a smile, in gracious manners, in beautiful speech is really the goodness which lies behind them. In mythology, the three Graces accompany Venus.

The fundamental meaning of the word "grace" is bound up with love. What pleases us, what we find agreeable, is what we love; but from the first form of love, which is an attraction to the loved object, we pass on to a higher form of love which is a "giving" to the being loved. The lover seeks what is pleasing to the beloved. Real love is always expressed by a giving and, above all, by a giving of one's self. The gift that comes from love, all that is generosity prompted by love, such is the deepest meaning of the word "grace". From this comes the idea of all that is given without its being the due of the recipient: of all that is purely a gift, of which a pardon, or remission of a punishment is only one particular and derived sense. So also we have the words "gratuitous", "gratuity", "gratuitously". What is gratuitous is pleasing because it is something given, and it is love that gives. The same meaning is to be found in the expression to be—or not—in someone's "good graces".

As for the aesthetic meaning of the word "gracious", or "graceful", it may be asked what grace adds to beauty, seeing that beauty is everything that pleases or attracts. It adds something in the nature of a giving of self. A beautiful woman is gracious when she has a manner of bearing herself, of behaving, that adds to her beauty. All that is gracious suggests something given or superadded, and beneath this external giving we sense the deep reality of love. Where there is no real love, there is only a false grace. The atheist can find only a counterfeit charm in nature unless he believes that it is the outcome of some divine generosity.

If we speak of the beauty of a flower, it is because we recognize in it some superabundance, for after all the reproduction of plants does not require such profusion, such luxuriance of forms and colours. There is no "grace", no charm, in what is necessary, or requisite, or owing, what is expected as a due, or the object of a bargain. Charm is always something in the nature of a superabundance. All poetry is beauty and reveals beauty, for over and above all rational knowledge it calls forth some superabundance of the mystery of things; and to what prose would say in a style that is grammatically correct, and logically precise, poetry adds something over and beyond: that is the grace of beautiful language. The words "charm" and "enchanting" suggest the same idea, for if grace is a gift it is, at the same time, an appeal; a call to receive; a call to open oneself to generosity and, finally, a call to love, to an exchange of love, and to *communion* in love.

As we understand the deeper meaning of the word "grace", we see that it always implies that human beings are not walled up, enclosed, imprisoned in themselves, in what separates them from others, with their exacting requirements and well-defined rights, but that there is intercourse and frankness between them: that they are open with one another, and there is some mutual self-giving one to another, and a sharing of something in common. The world of Sartre, with its abyss of nothingness between men, is a world without grace. Grace can be found only in a world of generosity. The Marxist world of struggle and hatred is a world without grace, for grace can be found only in a world where love is included in the very fundamental concepts of life, where even the existence of material things is a springing forth of love.

Grace is always to be found in this bursting forth of love, as in a spring that gushes out from an aperture in the ground, the opening of a flower, or the sudden breaking out of spring over a winter landscape. And grace is also a splendour—a glory, for there is no grace save in what is bestowed in profusion, like water, air, light, flowers in springtide, and like love, which is real only if it knows no measure. All aridity, avarice, miserliness, is opposed to grace. Visually, there is no longer any grace, once contours are arrested by too hard and straight a line. Grace always lets us suspect some endless prolongation, or some fusion in mutual exchange and communion. And that is why for reason, which reckons, defines and fixes boundaries, grace is something wonderful. There is no grace to be found in a world that is perfectly rational or logical, in the world of Descartes or Hegel; for grace always implies mystery, and always bears within it a hidden superabundance. That, then, is all we have been able to find out in the non-religious meanings and implications of the word "grace".

We thus reach the sense which the word "grace" bears in the vocabulary of religion. It can be found used in a childish or even superstitious religious sense, as when someone tells us that he has obtained "a grace" when a prayer has been answered. The meaning there is that God has granted something, given something; but in a real religion, that is, a disinterested love of God for himself, the word takes on a far deeper meaning, and it holds an essential place in the phraseology of the Judeo-Christian revelation.

In the Old Testament, we often read that the Jewish people, or some good man, or woman, *found grace with God*,[1] and the same expression is found again in the Gospel.[2]

The meaning is that the man or woman who has found grace in God's sight is pleasing to him and, at the same time, that God is bestowing upon him or her a gift, a benefit, and the important thing is that these two meanings are not simply in juxtaposition but inseparably connected. Left to himself, and to his own resources and potentialities, man is a sinner;

[1] Gen. 6. 8; 18. 3; 19. 19; 33. 10; 39. 4; 47. 29; 50. 4. Exod. 33. 12, 13, 17; 34. 9. 1 Kings 16. 22; 20. 3, 29; 27. 5. 2 Kings 14. 22; 15. 25. 3 Kings 11. 19. Ruth 2. 13. Judith 6. 17; 12. 17. Esther 2. 9; 5. 8; 7. 3; 8. 5. 1 Mach. 10. 60; 11. 24. Quotations in this chapter are from the Douay version, in the remaining chapters from the Knox version, unless otherwise stated.

[2] Luke 1. 30.

therefore he cannot merit the benefit of God, which, moreover, if it were merited would be man's due and hence not a pure gift. Sinful man cannot, of himself, be pleasing to God. For that, he must receive a gift from God which transforms him interiorly, cleanses him and sanctifies him by adorning him with qualities that render him pleasing to his Creator.

Already, then, we see grace not only as a pure gift of God, which man does not deserve and cannot obtain by himself, but as something which, once given, completely changes him, by purifying him inwardly from sin, and rendering him good and holy. By his grace, God communicates to man the holiness of which he is himself the fountain-head.

This first analysis enables us to avoid the great heresies of which we shall treat later—Pelagianism, since grace is shown to be a pure gift of God, which man cannot of himself obtain or merit, and the Lutheran and Calvinist heresies, since through this grace man ceases to be a sinner and is made truly virtuous and holy. The Old Testament well says that grace is the gift of God: *And I will give favour to this people*,[3] *And the Lord will give favour*[4]; *And the Lord gave favour to the people*.[5] To Judith it was said: *The God of our fathers give thee grace*.[6] But this grace or "favour" is really goodness and interior holiness. *He that is good, shall draw grace from the Lord*[7]; *the grace of God, and his mercy is with his saints*.[8] The most complete example in the Old Testament, although the actual word "grace" does not occur in it, is to be found in Ezechiel: "I will pour upon you clean water, and you shall be cleansed from all your filthiness, and I will cleanse you from all your idols. And I will give you a new heart, and put a new spirit within you."[9]

The fact remains that the exact and fundamental meaning

[3] Exod. 3. 21.
[4] Exod. 11. 3.
[5] Exod. 12. 36.
[6] Judith 10. 8.
[7] Prov. 12. 2.
[8] Wisdom 4. 15.
[9] Ezechiel 36. 25–6.

of these Old Testament texts can be grasped only because the New Testament has taught us to understand the full significance of the word "grace". Prepared by the former, the full revelation of the reality belongs to the latter. The Gospel, in particular, uses the word to express the work of God in Jesus Christ, who is stated to be "full of grace",[10] and as having the grace of God in him,[11] and in Mary, who is greeted as "full of grace". Thus it is the sanctity of Jesus and Mary that is the work of God. But it is in the teaching of St Paul that the word was used as a matter of course in the precise sense which came to be reserved for it in Catholic theology: that is, in the sense of a holiness which sinful man can neither have by any means of his own, nor merit by his works and his virtues, but which is given, or freely imparted to him, as a pure gift of God who, at the same time, both cleanses him and sanctifies him. For example, St Paul tells us that we are "justified freely by his grace",[12] and that we are "saved according to the election of grace, and if by grace it is not now by works: otherwise grace is no more grace".[13] To the Corinthians, he writes: "By the grace of God I am what I am",[14] and speaks to the Ephesians of "Christ, by whose grace you are saved . . . for by grace you are saved . . . and that not of yourselves, for it is the gift of God".[15] He reminds Timothy that "God has called us by his holy calling, not according to our own works, but according to his own purpose and grace".[16] And again: "To every one of us is given grace, according to the measure of the giving of Christ."[17] The same Apostle writes to Titus: "That being justified by his grace, we may be heirs according to the hope of life everlasting",[18] and again to the Ephesians that God has "predestinated us unto the praise of the glory of his grace, in which he hath graced us in his beloved Son".[19]

[10] John 1. 14.
[11] Luke 2. 40.
[12] Rom. 3. 24.
[13] *Ibid.* 11. 5–6.
[14] 1 Cor. 15. 10.
[15] Ephes. 2. 5–8.
[16] 2 Tim. 1. 9.
[17] Ephes. 4. 7.
[18] Titus 3. 7.
[19] Ephes. 1. 6.

Since the coming of our Lord, this grace constitutes the form of government of man's life, for the Apostle tells the Romans that we "are not under the law but under grace".[20] Such is the conception of grace which was taken up by the whole of Catholic tradition, and found its definitive expression with St Augustine and St Prosper, the Council of Orange and the condemnation of the Pelagian heresy. Then followed the theological developments due to St Bernard and St Thomas Aquinas, and the exact definitions of the Council of Trent against Luther and Calvin. Of that tradition, which we follow throughout our exposition, only two texts are here mentioned, one from St Thomas Aquinas, the Prince of Theologians, which says precisely: "Grace, inasmuch as it is gratuitously given, excludes the notion of debt",[21] and the other from one of the great mystics, St Catherine of Siena, who writes: "Why have we received so much grace? Is it on account of our virtue? No, but truly because of his infinite mercy." Thus we see that this Catholic tradition only develops a notion of grace which we have already found completely expressed in the teaching of St Paul.

We can now understand the use of the word "grace" and the fundamental rôle of the notion of grace in Catholic doctrine.

As we have seen, the religious meaning of the word may be applied to a quality whereby man is pleasing to God, or to a favour which God grants to men. The Pelagian heresy retained only the former sense, Luther and Calvin only the latter. But as we delve more deeply into the authentic meaning, we come to understand that these two senses are inseparable, and that we can only acknowledge both together. On the one hand, a man cannot be pleasing to God unless there is in him something like to God, something of the holiness of God, something that answers to the commandment our Lord gave in the

[20] Rom. 6. 14.
[21] *Summa. Theol.* 1a 2ae, q. 3, a. 1 ad 2.

Sermon on the Mount: "Be you perfect as your Father in heaven is perfect"; and that implies that God imparts to us something of himself, something of his divine sanctity, something not belonging to human nature, and to which man cannot attain by his own efforts. It is something freely given to man without previous merit on his part, in order to make him like to God and holy even with the holiness of God.

On the other hand, a gift from God does not come only from one who is rich, powerful and in a position to distribute all sorts of benefits but, as we shall see, from the author of our existence and that of all else, the source of all good and all perfection, from him who with respect to the creature is always the source of its being, its good, its perfection. Hence a gift from him ought to transform us interiorly, in our inmost being, enriching us with a new perfection, and if this gift really deserves to be called "grace" it is because here something is in question which is not owing to our human nature nor belonging to it, but received gratuitously, as a free gift; and so we reach the conception of a superhuman sanctity, truly divine, which God, by his grace, imparts to man.

The Catholic idea of grace is essentially of something which man, whatever his merits or efforts, is incapable of obtaining by himself: something which his human nature does not include and does not claim, and which is not due to him. Therefore, the word grace means that there is within us something infinitely superior to our human nature and to all our natural capacities, which for this reason is called "supernatural life", which designates the same reality as "grace", only that the latter word stresses the truth that we receive it freely without having merited it, that is, a gift springing from the pure generosity of God. The absolutely gratuitous nature of supernatural life is one of the most fundamental doctrines of the Catholic faith, and that is why the Church has always been particularly watchful against heresies such as that of Baius, and Immanentism which reject it. Quite recently, Pius XII spoke out strongly in the Encyclical *Humani Generis*, as did St Pius X, half a century ago, in *Pascendi*.

Certainly our very existence and our human nature are God's work and consequently God's gifts. But to what human nature carries with it naturally God, in his infinite generosity, has added that pure superabundance which is grace. When he created us, God gave us existence, understanding, will and all the natural perfections of man, but by his grace he gives himself. It is his own divine sanctity that he communicates to us. By creation God is Love which gives; by grace he is Love which gives himself. Grace is profusion, superabundant giving and generosity carried to the point of the gift of himself. The revelation of the mystery of grace shows us how infinite Love, that is God, is the gift of God himself, and that without measure.

Our reason cannot grasp such truths save according to human measure. Such a gift is a *mystery*, which we can know only through divine revelation. Our human intellect cannot form any idea of the divine sanctity that is in us by grace, and in which God himself is given to us, but we can believe it by faith.

We thus return to the fundamental basis: belief that God loves us because he has revealed it to us. What is at the source of grace is that infinite love of God carried to the point of his giving himself to us without measure. It is because God loves us that he bestows upon us a holiness whereby, being like to him, we are pleasing in his sight. To speak of "grace" and to speak of being loved by God is to use synonyms. To be "in a state of grace" is to be beloved of God. This comes out clearly if we think of that fullness of grace in Mary, in which we reaffirm our belief every time we say the *Ave Maria*. The two Latin words *gratia plena*, "full of grace", translate a single word in St Luke's original Greek, which word simply means that Mary is the object of the plenitude of divine love. The expression "Blessed art thou among women", which we add, is an excellent commentary, for the Archangel's words mean indeed that Mary is the most loved, the most cherished by God of all his creatures. To her God is given as completely as he could be, the fullness of his love overflows upon Mary. "Full of grace" means that she receives a love that is limitless. Perhaps the best translation of the Greek text of St Luke would be: "Rejoice, Mary, thou art the Beloved of God!"

But we shall see that Mary is the channel whereby infinite Love, made man in her, flows into all of us. The notion of grace means that we are the recipients of infinite Love, that we are the beloved children of God. And this infinite Love which thus gives itself we must receive by holding to it by our own love. By loving us, God calls us to love him. Grace is a call to love, a call to receive the love of which the initiative comes from God, a call to open our hearts to the divine generosity. Catholic revelation is a declaration on the part of God: a declaration of love for Mary through the words of the Archangel Gabriel at the annunciation, and subsequently a declaration of love to all mankind when the angels sang: "Peace on earth to those to whom God wills well." We may note here that the translation: "Peace to men of good will", is incorrect and near Pelagianism, if it meant that men could merit grace by their own good will. It is orthodox only if it is understood that man's good will is itself the work of grace. Even then it remains a mistranslation, for as is clear from the Greek text, there is no question here of the will. The sense is that it is God who, willing men's good, by loving them gives them that peace of which he is the author. By means of the angels, he proclaims peace to men because he wills their good: because he loves them. It is a proclamation of his love to all who receive it, and this proclamation the apostles and all the missionaries after them must cause to resound even to the ends of the earth. They have been sent by our Lord to teach men that God loves them, and they must draw near to all men to tell them that he does so.

Grace, then, is a call to an exchange of love between God and man, since it is a call to cling by love to that love God bears us. It brings about mutual love between him and ourselves—a communion of love between God and man. This Christian definition of grace, found in essence in the New Testament, has been progressively developed by Catholic tradition, and it is not superfluous to give here a very short historical account.

The problem of merit and predestination which, beginning with the period of Pelagius and St Augustine, occupied so important a place in the theology of grace was scarcely envisaged by the great Christian authors of the earlier centuries. The latter mention grace when treating of the sanctifying office of the Holy Spirit and of baptism; they emphasize the essential work of grace which is to make us members of Christ and, in him, the adopted children of the Father, deified by the Holy Spirit and thus made "to share the divine nature", to use St Peter's words,[22] to which we shall presently return. The first outstanding author whom we must cite is St Irenaeus, who inherits directly, through St Polycarp, the thought of St John. He tells us that God became Man in order that man might become a partaker of God,[23] "so that we may receive adoption through him",[24] "in order that we may recover in Jesus Christ what we have lost in Adam, that is, the image and likeness of God",[25] and that the "Holy Spirit may raise us up to the life of God".[26] St Irenaeus already distinguishes clearly between nature and grace, when he writes: "We are not created good

[22] 2 Peter 1. 4.

[23] *Contra Haereses*, 4, 28, 1. The Greek text with Latin translation will be found in Migne, *Patrologia Graeca* (hereinafter referred to as Migne, *P.G.*).

[24] *Ibid.* 3, 16, 3.

[25] *Ibid.* 18, 1.

[26] *Ibid.* 5, 9, 1.

in the beginning, but first men, and subsequently created gods."[27] Clement of Alexandria was the first to use the word "deify".

In the fourth century and before St Augustine, the problems of grace are to be found treated in connection with the exact definition of the doctrine of the Trinity. St Athanasius in his dispute with Arius, who denied the Godhead of the Word, is especially fond of developing the theme that the Word must, indeed, be God in order to be able to deify us by grace: that he must be the Son of God by nature so as to render us, in him, adopted children, a theme taken up again in the following century by St Cyril of Alexandria, in the discussion against Nestorius and when treating of the precise definition of the Incarnation. St Athanasius also brings out well the distinction between nature and grace when distinguishing between the creation which makes us creatures and the adoption which makes us children. This is to be found again in St Cyril of Jerusalem and St John Chrysostom. In the controversy against the Macedonians, who denied the deity of the Holy Spirit, St Basil, St Gregory Nazianzen, St John Chrysostom and St Cyril of Jerusalem develop the thesis that the Holy Spirit must indeed be God in order to have the power of deifying us by grace. St Basil defines grace when he says that "we become God",[28] and finally St Hilary and St Ambrose treat of grace when explaining the indwelling of the Blessed Trinity in the soul deified by grace.

In many passages, St Augustine repeated all the previous themes we have just summarized,[29] but he devotes the greatest portion of his considerable output on grace to maintaining the doctrine of St Paul against the Pelagian heresy, which was

[27] *Contra Haereses*, 4, 30, 4.

[28] *Liber de Spiritu Sancto*, IX, 23. Migne, *P.G.* t. 32.

[29] Here, for example, is a passage of his which admirably summarizes the whole earlier tradition: "God the Son, remaining in his own nature, became a sharer in our nature, so that remaining in our own nature we might be made sharers in his" (*Letter* 140, 10).

condemned in 418 by Pope Zosimus and the Council of Carthage. The whole theology of merit and predestination is elaborated in such works as the Treatises on *Grace and Free Will*, on *Nature and Grace*, on *The Grace of Christ and Original Sin*, on the *Predestination of the Saints* and on the *Gift of Perseverance*. Henceforth it was well established that of ourselves we cannot merit, as Pelagius claimed; that it is grace, a pure gift of God, which gives us our merits to which, nevertheless, we freely consent. We quote some very characteristic passages from St Augustine concerning this doctrine: "No man has anything of himself save lies and sin."[30] "Since all good things, be they great, medium or small, come from God, it follows that from God also comes the goodness of our free will."[31] "God works in man even the will to believe and it is always his mercy which forestalls us, but it belongs to the will to answer the divine call or reject it."[32] "Grace does not suppress free will but strengthens it, for grace cures the will whereby the good is loved."[33]

In the following century such leading spiritual writers as Cassian and St Vincent of Lérins fell into the error known as Semi-Pelagianism, by maintaining that if we cannot achieve our salvation alone without grace, as the Pelagians teach, yet the beginning of salvation may come from us alone, disposing and preparing us to receive grace. They were refuted by St Leo, St Prosper and St Caesarius, who maintained the well-established teaching of St Augustine, and in 529 the Council of Orange condemned Semi-Pelagianism by defining that even the beginning of the work of salvation is given by grace.

In the course of the succeeding centuries, the teaching of St Augustine found eminent continuators in St Leo, St Prosper and St Caesarius, already mentioned, and then in St Gregory

[30] *In Joannem*, 5, 1.
[31] *Retract.* I, 9, 6.
[32] *Treatise on the spirit and the letter*, 60.
[33] *Ibid.* 52.

the Great, St Isidore of Seville, St Bede and St Anselm. St Leo writes to the Bishop of Aquileia: "If grace is not something given, it is no longer a grace but a reward for our merits," and St Gregory writes:[34] "We must know that the only thing we possess of ourselves is evil. Good, on the contrary, comes from us but also from Almighty God who, by interior inspirations so forestalls us as to make us will, and then comes to our assistance so that we may not will in vain, but may be able to carry out what we will. Grace precedes, good will follow, and thus what is a gift of Almighty God becomes a merit that is our own." In his *Moralia*,[35] he writes again: "In the good deed, divine grace takes the initiative, and our free will follows." And again: "The good that we do is from God and from us: from God by prevenient grace, from us by our free good will." In St Isidore of Seville, we find: "Justification comes, at one and the same time, from God who gives it and man who receives it."[36] Finally, St Anselm says of God: "All our good things are thy gifts. We cannot serve and please thee unless thou dost give us so to do."[37]

Nevertheless, as the refutation of Pelagianism thus developed, there appeared contrary lines of thought preparing the way for the heresies of Calvin and Jansenius. These coalesced in the ninth century in the theory of Gottschalk on twofold predestination (to hell as well as to heaven) condemned at the Council of Quercy. In the twelfth century, the Pelagian theses, renewed by Abelard, were refuted by St Bernard who, with a masterly skill, summarized St Augustine's exposition, to be followed a century later by St Bonaventure.

In the thirteenth century, St Thomas Aquinas established theological science as a coherent and complete body of doctrine which, as Benedict XV says, "the Church has made her

[34] *In Ezechiel*, 1, Hom. 9, 2.
[35] *Moralia*, 24, 10 and 33, 40.
[36] *Sentences*, II, 5.
[37] *Meditations*, 18.

own" and then formed an orderly, well-fashioned and harmonious whole of the theology of grace, which was henceforth adopted as the whole official theology on the subject. This small work summarizes its essential features.

Unfortunately, as a consequence of the works of Occam, Biel and some others, the close of the Middle Ages was unfaithful to St Thomas, and Luther and Calvin encountered a doctrine of grace that had become deformed. Thus the Council of Trent found it necessary to restate the theology and give to the Catholic doctrine of grace its final, fixed formularies, thereby condemning the Lutheran and Calvinist heresies at the same time as those of Pelagius in the opposite direction. The seventeenth century saw the further condemnation of those of Baius and Jansenius, which constitute a kind of semi-Calvinism, and also that of Quesnel. This period was also concerned with the interminable controversies of the different theological schools, which space forbids our studying in this book.

Thus beginning with an analysis of Catholic phraseology, we have been able to fix the essential and historical meaning of the doctrine of grace. We must now expound the Catholic meaning of grace in a connected and orderly manner.

Since grace is something far beyond man's natural capacities, we can explain precisely what the supernatural life of grace is only after we have considered his natural potentialities in order to show how far grace surpasses them. Therefore, we must begin with a preliminary chapter on the possibilities and limits of human nature. The philosophical nature of this chapter will, perhaps, make it arduous for the reader, but what follows will show its necessity. We shall then explain exactly what is meant by supernatural life, and this forms the basis of the whole doctrine of grace in the next chapter, dealing with God's gift to man, or sanctifying grace.

Not only is this sanctifying grace given to us initially, but it is preserved, increased and maintained in us to the moment of our death only by that divine action in us which we call actual grace. Moreover, this divine action may be already working in us to prepare the way for sanctifying grace before the latter is bestowed upon us. Consequently, in order to learn the conditions under which supernatural life exists in us, a further chapter will be needed in which we consider God's action in us, or actual grace.

It then remains for us to study Jesus Christ as the source whence grace comes to us. We shall see how sinful man cannot escape from his condition as such save only through the perfect and superabounding reparation for sin made by our Lord on the cross; so that for mankind, issuing from Adam and Eve, he is the one and only source of all grace. Therefore we must know how this grace flows into us through the sacraments, and how the Church, that organism of grace, is constituted. The fifth chapter will therefore consider Christ, the one and only source of grace.

From this we can conclude that the entire spiritual life of the Catholic is but the flowering, the developing of the life of grace, and that without grace at its source there is no real spiritual life.

And this is the subject of our concluding chapter, "A Spirituality of Grace".

CHAPTER II

THE ENDOWMENTS AND LIMITS OF HUMAN NATURE

KNOWLEDGE

In common with the animals, man possesses an extraordinary perfection which distinguishes them from lifeless beings and from plants: this is the power of knowing. A being not endowed with knowledge is strictly limited to itself, as it were, enclosed and imprisoned in itself, without any outlook upon the rest of the world, and without any communication with other beings, who are to it as though they did not exist. A being endowed with knowledge has access to the rest of the world by knowing it, and is in communication with everything that it knows. Further, our acts of knowledge are something belonging to us, and what we know is present in our act of knowledge. Consequently, all the beings we know are truly present in us in the knowledge that we have of them. The word "know" has no sense without a subject and a complement, called the object. The subject is what knows and the object what is known; thus it can be stated precisely that knowledge is the presence of the object known in the subject knowing. It is not a material but an immaterial presence; and this kind of presence belongs so properly to the case of knowledge that it cannot be compared to any other form of presence, for the subject knows only by possessing in itself the presence of the object in the knowledge it has thereof.

Hence, to know is, in a certain manner, to possess in oneself all one knows: to enrich one's own being with the being of all one thus knows, possessed thus in oneself, and through the knowledge which one has of it. We can understand, therefore, what an extraordinary perfection knowledge is, since a being endowed with it, far from being limited to its own self, is through its knowledge enriched with the presence and possession within it of all that it knows. Consequently, knowledge is the great means of communication between beings, of their intercourse with one another. Whereas beings without knowledge are absolutely shut in, separated, beings endowed with knowledge can communicate their being in such wise that in knowing one another they are present in one another, each possessing in himself the others by knowing them. The being who knows enlarges its own being in the measure of all it knows, possessed in it through knowledge. So it is that knowledge is an increase, an enrichment, a perfection of being, and we shall see that only a being endowed with knowledge can receive supernatural life.

The animal's means of knowing is limited to what can be acquired through the senses. It knows the outward world by means of the physical action exercised by that world upon its organs by such phenomena as light, sound and heat; so that its knowledge is extremely restricted owing to the fact that it cannot be acquired without physical action exercised upon its sense organs. The sight knows only the light acting upon the eyes, and so knows luminous objects; the hearing knows only what acts upon the ears, and thereby it knows the objects that emit a sound, etc. So the senses know only the physical properties of things—contour, sound, smell, etc.

INTELLECT

Man possesses sensitive knowledge in common with the animals, but what distinguishes him from all the other animal species, and defines his human nature, is that he possesses in addition another and superior form of knowledge, quite distinct from that acquired through the senses, which is intellect, intelligence or understanding. By his intelligence man knows the *nature* of things. For example, by seeing, I know the colours of a man's hair and eyes; by hearing, I know the sound of his voice and of his steps; but by means of the *idea* of man which my intelligence conceives and grasps I know his human nature. When I know an object through the senses, I can describe it by its physical and sensible characteristics: colour, sound, smell, etc. When through intellect I have the idea of an object, I can define it, that is, I can explain *what it is*, because I know its nature. And it is because the intellect thus knows the nature of things that man can invent, make progress, foresee and organize.

Sensitive knowledge grasps the exterior aspect of things through attaining to their external, physical characteristics by means of the physical action exercised by light, sound, heat, etc., but the gaze of the intellect penetrates to their interior, to discover in them what constitutes them in their innermost being: what they are, that is, what we call their nature. The very word "intelligence" means this look which penetrates within beings and lights them up interiorly.

For all that, in the unity of the human being sensitive knowledge and intellect, though distinct, are neither separated from nor independent one from the other. It is a fact that at his birth man has in him no *idea*, no intellectual knowledge of what some philosophers have called "the innate"; but gradually, as our eyes see, our ears hear, our hands feel, as we come to know the exterior world through the senses, our intellect forms in itself ideas and we acquire intellectual knowledge. All that is drawn from experience gained through the senses; all the history of human thought proves that the latter makes progress and comes to know the world better and better, only through learning in the school of experience: the one and irreplaceable point of departure of all intellectual activity. We may even add that all of which we have no experience is inconceivable to us; we can have no idea of it.

We must conclude, therefore, that human intelligence knows nothing directly, for it has no direct contact with the reality to be known. We have direct contact with the outward reality only through the action exercised by light, sound, heat, etc., upon our sensitive organs. But once sensitive experience has thus brought us into contact with the reality to be known, whereas the senses themselves know only colours, sounds, smells, physical phenomena, the eye of the intellect penetrates through this evidence of sensitive experience to the nature of the reality to be known: to what constitutes it in its very being, and it is thus that our ideas and intellectual notions by the activity of the intellect are extracted or, as we commonly say, "abstracted" from the evidence supplied by experience: from the contact established by experience with the reality to be known.

A very important consequence for the remainder of this book is that everything not attainable by means of sensitive experience, everything therefore that is immaterial or spiritual, is absolutely and forever incomprehensible to human understanding which cannot, and never can, form the least idea of such, since we cannot conceive of that of which we have no experience. Therefore there exists for our intellect a region of mystery, or darkness, which remains impenetrable for ever so long as we remain limited to our natural capacities.[1]

Another consequence is that our intellectual activity is not

[1] We shall see later that our idea of God knows him indirectly through the medium of his works, but does not attain him in himself.

limited to the formation of ideas. An idea, because it is abstract, never knows the whole of any reality whatever, but only some intelligible aspect of that reality. For example: by the idea "man", I know the human nature of Peter, but I do not know the "whole" Peter, whence comes the necessity of multiplying ideas. When I know that Peter is a man, I have still to know that he is free (the idea of liberty), that he is a musician (the idea of aptitude for music), etc. Therefore, it is necessary to connect ideas with one another, when they enable us to know different aspects of the same reality. That is the work of the judgement. Thus, I am forming a judgement when I say that a man is a musician, or that he is free. By the judgement, the intellect pronounces upon the reality to be known by affirming or denying. The judgement is not valid intellectual knowledge unless it conforms to the reality to be known: that is, unless it is true. Truth is the essential quality of judgements.

The judgement itself is still partial. After having put the ideas together in the judgement, for example the ideas of "man" and "freedom", they must be linked one to another and made to follow one another in reasoning. We thus see how the acquisition of our intellectual knowledge is a long, difficult and progressive task; since after having explored the reality by experience and formed ideas by abstraction, we must bind up the ideas together in the judgement and link the judgements together in the reasoning.

Human intelligence is thus partial, successive and progressive. It is partial because it never knows the total reality all at once, successive because our partial items of knowledge must follow one another in order to become complete, and progressive because in this succession of ideas there is enrichment or progress. We express all this by saying that human intelligence is *discursive*, as a discourse which progresses by being composed of successive portions; and this knowledge which knows, one after another, the different aspects of the real, in a manner that is multiple and divided, is opposed to a knowledge that is "intuitive", of which only pure spirits are capable. Intuitive knowledge attains and takes in at a glance the totality of a reality, which is grasped at once in all its aspects, because the intelligence of a pure spirit does not depend upon sense perceptions, but knows directly without having to extract its knowledge from experience.

These characteristics of the human understanding involve the possibility of error, if we put the ideas together in our judgement wrongly, in a manner not conforming to the reality. If, for example, we joined together the idea of a stone and the idea of life, by saying that a stone is alive, we should be wrongly connecting the judgements in the reasoning process.

Notwithstanding this risk of error, there are two cases in which we may be absolutely certain of the truth: firstly, when, thanks to the evidence of experience, we state what we have received directly from experience: what, for instance, we have seen with our own eyes. It was thus that the apostles affirmed the fact of our Lord's resurrection. The second case is when we state a conclusion demonstrated by strict reasoning, and we shall see that such is the case for affirming the existence of God.

Consequently, notwithstanding the possibility and risk of error, there are cases when we can be certain of the truth. On the other hand, if the error is only a risk or an accident, ignorance is inevitable and is always there to limit our intellectual knowledge. It is the result of that knowledge being, as we have said, partial, successive and progressive, that it is never complete: that we shall always be finding out something new: that it is always limited, incomplete—although certain in that which it can affirm—that we never know the whole of any reality whatever; that the inexhaustible wealth and complexity of the reality always exceeds the knowledge we have of it; that there is in the reality a superabundance which our intellectual knowledge will penetrate better and better as it makes progress, but will never be able to exhaust. As Shakespeare tells us in *Hamlet*, "there are more things in heaven and earth . . . than are dreamt of in (our) philosophy."

Such are the possibilities and limits of our human nature in the order of knowledge. Let us now see what they are in the order of action.

WILL, FREEDOM AND MORAL LIFE

Every imperfect being tends to perfect itself, and therefore carries within it inclinations towards the perfection which it lacks. Everything that can, in some way or another, make a being more perfect, is called a "good". The word is here taken in its most general sense, of every object of an inclination: everything towards which one can tend and not in the more restricted sense of a moral good, which we shall define later. Thus, in every being there are these inclinations towards what is a "good", and they lead beings to "act", to enter into activity, in order to obtain the good towards which they tend, and that is why the universe is in perpetual activity, in incessant transformation. The "good" which an activity tends to obtain is called its object (though this object is conscious only in beings endowed with knowledge), or its "end", because the activity that has obtained its object, or end, is finished or terminated.

In beings endowed with knowledge there are inclinations towards known good things: inclinations that result from knowing the good objects towards which they are tending. The first of these inclinations, and the source of all the others, is love which is the basis and the first mover of all the activities of such beings. They act because they tend towards what they love. Love develops and expands into joy in the possession of the object loved, or into suffering owing to being deprived of it. Like the word "know", the word "love" makes no sense without a subject and an object. All love postulates a subject that loves and an object that is loved. And love, although in a very different manner from knowledge, postulates also a presence of the object loved in the subject that loves.

The object is present, not materially but in a manner proper to the movement of love, in the subject that loves by the attraction that draws the subject to the object. Love is therefore, though differently from knowledge, a great means of communication and union between things. Through love, beings that tend one towards another are present in one another through the attraction which draws them together; and so are, in a way, placed and drawn out of themselves, made to go beyond their limits, by being given to one another. The being that loves goes forth from itself in a movement that draws it out of itself, in order to give itself to the being loved.

Among all animals, men included, we find inclinations that tend towards good as known through the senses. These are the feelings, the emotions, the passions, and are produced by the functioning of the organism, the state of the nerves and of the glands. We are not responsible for them, and consequently there is neither merit nor demerit in what we experience or feel. We have no choice as regards them and they do not depend upon us. The merit or the fault begins with responsibility, that is with consent. This amounts to saying that throughout this domain of the sensitive inclinations, there is no freedom, for freedom is the power of choice. In order to choose, we must compare: to compare, we must judge, and to form a judgement is an act of the intelligence. Hence, freedom, as we shall explain more precisely, results from the intervention of the intellect which forms a judgement, and is in no way connected with the activity of the senses, which is wholly determined by the condition of the organism. Those who think they are free when they do everything they like, that is, when they obey their passions blindly, are really automatons, led from within by the functioning of their nerves and their glands, and are not free at all.

However, man is not led only by his sensitive inclinations. His activity depends also upon the inclination resulting from the intellect, whereby he turns towards the good known by means of the latter. When he turns to something because his understanding has judged it to be good and he is following this judgement, we say that he wills it, and that is why we call the inclination towards what the intellect judges to be good the *will*.

Because, by forming judgements, the intellect is able to compare good things with one another, the will can choose and it is that power of choosing which we call *freedom*. Thus the intellect enables a man by knowing the object of his acts, and himself directing them to their object, to reason and govern his life and conduct: to be master of his own acts and consequently responsible for them. But a man is not making use of his freedom when he acts without reflection, by blindly following his passions. He acts voluntarily and freely only if he reflects before he acts, in order to judge with his intellect as to what makes for his good, and decide in consequence with his will. Freedom is power to decide concerning his acts, guided by the judgement which furnishes the motives for them.

This power of himself deciding what he will do, because he is capable of forming judgements and thus of guiding himself, of being his own master, is a great perfection of man. But, like the human intelligence of which it is a consequence, human freedom is limited. Firstly, just as human intelligence depends upon the senses, human freedom is influenced by the feelings, the emotions and the passions, and this influence of our sensitive movements sets limits to our freedom. In reality, acts that are perfectly free because they are perfectly independent of all influence of the feelings, are exceptional. Usually, human acts are imperfectly free, more or less free, and therefore more or less responsible according to the influence and allurement exercised by the passions and unconscious psychological mechanisms. Moreover, the discursive character of the human intelligence causes the slowness of the freedom to decide, after the long and progressive work of deliberation, whereby an individual successively weighs the pros and cons. Deliberation ends in decision, because then the will freely chooses by giving its preference to the decisive motive which the final judgement takes alone into consideration, putting aside the contrary motives; and it is by this adhesion to the decisive motive that we bind our freedom and our responsibility. Consequently, it is the decisive motive which gives value to the wilful free act. As a result of this, human freedom is unstable: that is, it can reverse its decisions, repent of them, since it is always possible, after having decided, to begin deliberating again and take the contrary decision.

An unintelligent being cannot know the object of its acts, therefore cannot choose and decide what it will do, and so cannot guide itself. It is guided automatically by its nature and thus all its activities are governed by laws which it obeys without knowing or willing them, and to which it cannot choose to conform or not to conform. There are the physical laws which govern all mechanical, physical, chemical and physiological phenomena, as also the sense life of both animals and men. But our free acts are not governed by physical laws because we can choose; or, to speak more exactly, the outward performance of the act obviously depends upon physical laws, but what is free, namely the interior act of decision, does not. This domain of man's voluntary acts, this realm of free decisions, or of his free and responsible behaviour, constitutes therefore in the universe a world apart, which we call "the moral order", from the word "morals"; this is the domain of human moral conduct.

If this moral region is not governed by the physical laws, it must have laws of another kind which we call "moral laws". Such laws do not make us act without knowing or willing, by means of a natural automatism, but make us act voluntarily by working from the knowledge we have from them. By means of his intellect, man knows what is necessary for his welfare; this knowledge which should rule our acts is a moral law: therefore a law which we obey voluntarily, knowing and willing it. We can conform to it, and then our good will result. That act, freely directed to our true welfare, of which that welfare is the decisive motive on which we have decided after rejecting all contrary motives, is the *morally good* act, a responsible act by which we merit our true good which results from it.

We are able, also, not to follow the moral law: to decide to turn away from our true advantage, to refuse to do what is necessary to guide us thereto, and then instead of making ourselves more perfect we degrade ourselves, diminish ourselves, suffer privation of good or of perfection. Such consequences are deserved by the act which is morally bad, for which we are responsible since by it we freely turn aside from our true advantage; we reject from our decision the motive of our true welfare by deciding for the contrary motives.

Hence the moral law is not a "regulation", a system of permissions and prohibitions imposed upon us from without, but an interior law resulting from the very nature of the intelligent being, by which the latter knows what is for his good and turns to it. Moral sanctions are no longer rewards or punishments assigned from outside, like a sweet or a chastisement to a child, but they are the actual consequence, for good or evil, of the free decisions for which we are responsible. Evil is not a matter of a forbidden good, but a privation of good or of perfection. The moral law does not diminish our freedom, since it must be obeyed freely. It protects that unsteady freedom, constantly liable, as it is, to disappear when we blindly yield to our passions: it increases our freedom, because it trains us to act freely by following the judgement of our intellect. But it is because our human freedom is imperfect that it thus needs a law to protect and perfect it. Since the moral law is not imposed from without, what constitutes the moral value of an act is not the outward execution of it but, as we have said, the inner motive of the decision: the deep-seated energy of the will, freely leading it to the choice of our true good, or to its rejection.

For that reason, we cannot judge of the moral value of other people, because we do not see into their consciences. Since it belongs to the moral law to direct our acts through the knowledge we have of it, it binds us only in the measure in which we know it. In the case of involuntary ignorance or error there is no sin, because sin lies only in knowingly turning away from what is good. Now here, as everywhere, ignorance is possible, for the human intellect acquires its knowledge of the moral law only slowly, with difficulty and progressively, as it does all knowledge.

Thus therefore, there is nothing arbitrary about the moral laws; they exist only for the true good to which they guide us. Our moral life requires us to conform to these laws only that we may obtain what is for our good. The laws are only means, only roads to follow, in order to reach the goal, but the nature of the moral life is not to be found in conforming to rules but in the dynamism aiming at the true good known through the intellect.

Moreover, there is a hierarchy, a subordination, in all the good things or perfections which a man may seek, but this hierarchy can exist only because there is an Absolute Good, desired by man in an absolute manner, and which he subordinates to no other but to which he subordinates everything else. All our desires exist only because of a desire that takes first place, is radical, fundamental, whereby man wills something absolutely and everything else for the sake of that something. This end to which all others are subordinated, and at which the hierarchy of ends stops, is known as our *last end*. For the miser it is money, for a follower of Hitler it was German supremacy, for a Christian it is God. The last end is the motive of the morally good act, because the moral life means the orientation of the will to that last end.

THE SPIRITUAL AND IMMORTAL SOUL

Having described human capacities and their limits, we must still see how man is constituted.

Every corporal being consists of matter, but the living being does not owe its life to the matter of which it is made, since the corpse consists of the same matter yet no longer has life. This means that in the living being the matter is organized by a life-principle, by something that makes it living, and this is called the soul. In the vegetable world, it is an organic soul, which gives plants organic life, and in the animals a sensitive soul, which gives them sensation at the same time. This vegetable or animal soul cannot exist without the material organs, which it animates, so that with death it disappears.

But the human soul, in order to give man all that belongs to his nature as such, gives him not only organic and sentient life but also intelligence and the freedom resulting therefrom. It is an intellectual and free soul, organizing the matter of which we are made into a human body, having life, sensibility and thought. Now the intellect is immaterial or spiritual, because the thought that is its work is, as we have seen, the presence within us of all that we know of the known reality. But it is not a material presence and it is therefore immaterial or spiritual, and such also is the case with the intellect that thinks. Pascal has well expressed this: "All bodies, the firmament, the stars, the earth and its realms, are not worth the least of the spirits, for the spirit knows all that and itself and the bodies nothing. . . . From all bodies together, we could not succeed in extracting the slightest thought; that is impossible and belongs to another order." We must conclude, then, that the human soul, endowed with the immaterial faculties of intellect and will, capable of spiritual acts of thought and love, is itself immaterial and spiritual.

Consequently, man possesses a human nature only because his body is organized into a human body: that is, a body which not only lives and feels but thinks and wills by means of a spiritual soul. However, that spiritual soul is not, as Plato and Descartes held, a pure spirit which, being an independent spiritual substance, is a kind of "double" to the body, enclosed or imprisoned in the latter; on the contrary, it is the organizing and animating principle of the body which, by making it a human body, constitutes with it the single and individual substance of man in his unity. That is why our spiritual life, both intellectual and moral, depends upon the sensitiveness and state of the body and its organs which are animated by the soul.

It is human nature which requires a soul that is spiritual, the latter therefore is natural to man and has nothing supernatural about it. It would be a serious error to confuse the natural spirituality of the human soul with the supernatural life of grace which is the subject of this book. Again, it is absurd to speak of the soul, the intellect or free will as the "divine spark"; for the soul that gives us human nature is human and in no way divine. It is the supernatural life of grace, and that alone, which is divine.

The fact that, unlike the souls of plants and animals, the human soul is immaterial, involves the consequence that it is immortal. Death is a change undergone by the matter of the body, which ceases to be organized by the soul and becomes the matter of a corpse. This change cannot destroy a soul which of its own nature is immaterial, and so independent of matter.

When the soul ceases at death to organize the body, the former finds itself in a state that is purely spiritual. That is why there is something deeply mysterious about the immortal life of the soul after death: something obscure, even inconceivable, of which we can form no idea since, as has been said, we can conceive only that of which we have experience. What we call "the beyond" is, to human intelligence, an impenetrable mystery.

We are able, nevertheless, to think that after death a soul that is both spiritual and intellectual will have in itself all that is necessary to know itself, to comprehend itself, with all that is in it, with a complete knowledge perfectly clear and lucid of itself; for if the greater portion of ourselves is incapable of knowing, and our knowledge extremely limited so long as the soul organizes the body, we have seen that this is so because the intellect is in a state of dependence upon the senses, which compel it to extract all its information from sensitive experience. Hence, far from being a sleep, death is the awakening of the soul to full knowledge of itself. The intellect, being now no longer obliged to extract its knowledge from experience, ceasing to be discursive becomes intuitive; it is itself, whole and entire, with all that is in it, that the soul embraces and seizes upon in a single gaze, as well as all the data of its destiny.

No longer is there any examination by stages of pros and cons, therefore no longer is there any deliberation which could be repeated. This means that freedom becomes stable, being no longer able to reverse its decisions or repent of them through beginning to deliberate over again. Therefore, the decision taken at the moment of death, with a freedom that has in this way become stable, and thus cannot change, is an irrevocable, final decision, of which we shall never repent because we are fully, totally committed.

THE KNOWLEDGE OF GOD

We have said what man can know of the world and himself. Can our knowledge carry us further? Since the intellect knows the natures of things and therefore can understand the universe, it can understand that the universe, not being self-existent, receives existence from a First Cause which we call God. But there can be no question of a direct knowledge of God, such as would attain to him in himself, in his divine reality: firstly, because the human intellect cannot grasp what is immaterial and spiritual and, secondly and especially, because no finite and limited intellect, be it our own or that of the angels, can attain to and comprehend the Being who is infinite and perfect. God is an impenetrable mystery not to be attained by any finite and limited intelligence, angelic or human. That is why the Church has condemned all the theories which have laid claim to a direct knowledge of God: the ontology of Malebranche and Rosmini and, in more recent times, the Immanentism which holds that we can become aware of the presence of God in us by some "religious experience", or "religious sense".[2] It is evident that there can be no experience whereby God would be naturally perceived by us.

There can, therefore, be question only of an indirect knowledge of God, that is to say a knowledge acquired through some intermediary. But such indirect knowledge can be perfectly accurate and certain as when, for example, a cause which cannot be directly known is known indirectly by means of its effects, if it is a question of effects that cannot exist without that cause. Such is exactly the case where God is concerned. St Paul tells us that the "men have caught sight of his invisible nature, his eternal power and his divineness, as they are known through his creatures",[3] and the Vatican Council has defined that it is by this way of causation that "the existence of God may be known by the natural light of reason".

Many examples might be cited of an indirect and absolutely certain knowledge of a cause from its effects. When I see the

[2] See the Encyclicals *Pascendi* of St Pius X and *Humani Generis* of Pius XII.

[3] Romans 1. 20.

hands of my watch, I am certain of the existence of the mechanism which I do not see, because without the latter the hands could not move. When I see a footprint in sand, I am absolutely sure that a person whom I have not seen has passed by; that person whom I do not know directly is known indirectly from the footprints left on the sand. So is the Creator known indirectly from the existence of the creatures who could not exist unless they received that existence from him.

It is because the hands of the watch cannot move by themselves that we can affirm that they receive the power to move from a cause of movement, which is the mechanism. It is because the sand has not in itself the power to produce the footprint, that we can state that it has received the impression from the foot of someone who has passed by. Likewise, it is because creatures are not self-existent that they cannot have existence unless they receive it from an existential cause which we call God.

How do we know that creatures do not derive existence from themselves? If the hands of the watch moved by themselves they would always be in movement. If the sand possessed in itself the form of a human foot, it would have it always and everywhere. If a being is self-existent, it is unable not to exist, that is, it exists always. Such is not the case with creatures, every one of which has had a beginning. Moreover, even if we supposed a universe that had no beginning, that is to say that there was always something in existence, it would still remain true that every one of the beings that make up the universe had a beginning. Further, if a being were self-existent, that is, if it did not receive existence from an outside source, nothing could limit it. It would be infinite and perfect, and such is obviously not the case with creatures, every one of which is finite and limited. It follows with absolute certainty that creatures do not exist of themselves, which necessarily means that they receive existence from the Cause of all existence.

The Cause of existence, which is the source whence all existence arises, and explains everything that exists, cannot itself receive existence; therefore God is the self-existent Being, that is to say the necessary Being. He cannot not exist, which means that he exists always, that he is eternal and nothing can limit his existence in any respect whatsoever. Therefore he is the infinite and perfect Being.

From this, there follow some important consequences:

1. God is immaterial, for all that is made from matter is limited by that matter.

2. God is unique, because were there two Gods each would have something lacking in the other and they would not be perfect.

3. God is changeless, for only an imperfect being can change, by acquiring something that is lacking to it. The perfect being can acquire nothing and therefore cannot change. But only change causes the diversity of moments, one after another: therefore in God there is no succession of moments, that is to say no time. Divine eternity is thus whole and entire in a single moment, which we cannot understand any more than we can understand God himself. This explains how things are only past or future with respect to us, who are in time, but that everything is present in the single moment, the endless "now" of divine eternity. We express this imperfectly when we say that God foresees the future; he "sees" it because to him the future is present.

4. God possesses every perfection in an infinite degree. He is infinite goodness, infinite beauty, etc. Among these perfections, there are two upon which it behoves us to insist, in view of what follows in this book, when the study of grace will involve our mentioning them frequently: on the one hand, God is infinite and perfect intellect, and on the other perfect will and freedom, that is, perfect love.

First, if the perfect Being is, for all limited intelligence, impenetrable darkness, he cannot be so for himself: for him, there can be no darkness, nothing obscure. The perfect Being is necessarily for himself perfectly clear, luminous, transparent; otherwise he would not be perfect. God is, then, an act of perfect understanding of himself. The perfect Being, wholly luminous for himself, cannot but be perfect penetration, perfect comprehension of himself, and that is what St John expresses by saying that God is Light.

It follows necessarily that the infinite Being loves himself perfectly; otherwise he would not be infinite and perfect. Therefore, God is an act of perfect love of himself. Just as he is an eternal light of knowledge, so is he an eternal flame of love. The perfect Being can only perfectly possess and perfectly embrace himself in total love: the gift of love to himself, expressed by St John when he says that God is Love. And if God is the perfect Being, penetrating himself, and understanding himself, loving and possessing himself perfectly, he is absolute, infinite and perfect joy.

There we have what, without understanding anything of the unfathomable mystery of an infinite and perfect Being, without knowing anything of what God is in himself in his divine reality, our human intellect can, by its natural means, know of the Creator through the medium of the creatures to which he gives existence.

THE CONDITION OF THE CREATURE

To affirm that there is a Creator is not only to reject atheism but also to reject pantheism, which ignores the distinction between God and the universe by holding that the latter is something of God, like an emanation, a transformation or an appearance. Between the one infinite and perfect Being, simple and unchangeable, and finite, limited and imperfect creatures, multiple and changeable, the distinction is absolute. Thus to affirm the Creator is, first, to affirm that God gives to beings distinct from himself a real existence distinct from his own. Man cannot cause anything to exist but can merely transform what exists already; to give existence, to create, belongs to God.

To affirm the Creator is also to affirm that nothing can exist unless it receives its being from God, and therefore that God is the total cause of the totality of the being of the creature, that there is nothing in the being of the creature that does not come from him. Therefore the creature is constituted in its very being by this radical, absolute, total dependence upon God, from whom it receives its being and all that is implied thereby.

It follows from this that nothing is produced, even in the smallest details, without depending upon this universal causality of God which nothing escapes. That is what we express when we say that God is Providence. Must we conclude from this, with the fatalists, that if God does everything creatures do nothing? This is a very important problem, which has serious consequences in the doctrine of grace. Unquestionably experience proves to us that, against all fatalism, creatures do exercise an action, and that a very real one. But this action, like everything created, has no existence of itself, but exists only because God gives it existence. Thus all divine causality, far from suppressing the action of creatures, brings it into existence. His causality and that of the creature are not two exterior forces, one added to the other, like two horses drawing a carriage, in which case if one does all the other does nothing. It is interiorly, in the action exercised by the creature that there is to be found, at the very source of its being, the causality of God that causes it to exist. It has been claimed that such a doctrine suppresses human freedom; but that is a serious misunderstanding, since human freedom is a creature that does not exist of itself but only by receiving existence from God. Consequently, the divine causality, far from suppressing our freedom, causes it to exist. What would suppress our freedom would be a causality acting upon the latter from outside, but it is within our freedom that is to be found, at the very source of its being, the divine causality which makes it exist as it is, that is, *free*. That is why St Paul could write to the Philippians: "Both the will to do it and the accomplishment of that will are something which God accomplishes in you, to carry out his loving purpose."[4]

Therefore, God is the source of all good things and of all perfection but, on the other hand, he is in no way the cause of evil, for evil is merely the lack or privation of good and perfection and so a privation of being. Now it is clearly what exists that requires God as the cause of existence. The lack or privation does not need a cause of existence, and in no way comes from God. As we shall see presently, it is a serious mistake and a widespread one to draw a parallel between the case of the good, which is truly positive, and that of the evil, which is negative, being merely lack or absence.

It remains to see why God created, seeing that he is perfectly self-sufficing in his infinite perfection to which nothing is wanting. He is in no way obliged to create, for creation adds nothing to him who needs nothing. God, who is infinite freedom, is absolutely free to create or not to create. Hence creation, which brings nothing to him, is on his part purely gratuitous, pure generosity, a pure gift to the creature of everything that it has within it. Being, good, perfection, and therefore creation is a pure act of love, purely the overflow or superabundance of love. God creates in order to give, because he is infinite generosity and love.

Thus we end our consideration of the possibilities and limits of human nature. Because he is a creature, man is utterly dependent upon God, who dwells in his deepest being, as the very source of his existence, and notwithstanding this he is separated from his creature by an infinite distance, an abyss that cannot be crossed, which divides the imperfect and limited creature from the infinite and perfect Being. Any in-

[4] Phil. 2. 13.

timacy, any familiarity, any personal relations with God seem impossible to man. We know God as the Creator through the medium of creatures, without knowing anything of the unfathomable mystery of what he is in his divine reality. We can, and ought, then, to love him because of his gifts, as the source of all that is in us that is good and perfect; but we cannot love him in himself and for himself. We can speak to him as our creator, but the idea could never occur to us of calling him our Father, were there nothing in us that exceeds our natural capacities. What our soul's immortal life will be after death, what is the object of human history, of mankind and of the universe, how all the accumulated evil in that history can minister to some higher good—all these are insoluble enigmas for our human intellect, which knows nothing of God's purposes.

From this condition of human nature, false religions and false mysticism—everything that is a *gnosis*, or natural mysticism—claim to enable us to escape by a human effort which, of itself and by itself, thanks to suitable methods or technique, would raise us to God. That is impossible. What we are is determined by our human nature, and man cannot, of himself and by himself, escape from the limitations of his nature. To these dangerous illusions we oppose the Christian doctrine of grace, that is of the pure gift of God, which depends upon him alone, and which we can only receive.

CHAPTER III

SANCTIFYING GRACE

TRUTH KNOWN NATURALLY AND TRUTH REVEALED

When we examined the capacities and limitations of human nature, we saw that by his human nature man is endowed with means of acquiring knowledge which are experience and reasoning; so that there is a whole sphere of truths which he is naturally capable of knowing. There are scientific and philosophical truths, and among the latter we can include the spirituality and immortality of the human soul and the existence of God, who is the Creator and known as the Cause of the existence of creatures. But we saw also that this field of truths thus naturally knowable is limited, and that beyond it there is another domain which cannot be known by the human intellect, which constitutes for the latter an insoluble mystery, a region of which we should never be able to know or find out anything by our natural powers. We can never know what the immortal life of our soul after death will be like, what God is in himself in his divine reality, his purposes in the history of creation as a whole. Of this mysterious region we can know something only if God himself, who alone knows it, speaks to us to teach us what we can never learn for ourselves.

We could have no idea that this might be possible, did not the real history of the human race confront us with the fact that it has effectively taken place. The essential fact of all human history is that God has intervened personally and directly in that history, in order to speak to us by means of patriarchs and prophets, of Jesus Christ and of the Church, and thus teach us what God alone knows. Moreover, we have the guarantee that such is the case because that intervention is accompanied by a whole group of facts (prophecies, miracles, holy lives, etc.) which could only be the work of divine omnipotence. Such is the fundamental fact of our history which constitutes revelation. The mysteries which our human intellect could never have discovered have been revealed to us in what God himself has taught us through the patriarchs, the prophets, Christ and the Church, which serves him as the instrument whereby to speak to us in human language which we can understand.

First, during the succeeding ages of the patriarchs and prophets, there was a revelation that was partial, provisional, gradual and progressive. In Jesus Christ who, as we shall see, is God himself made Man, is revealed the mystery of God in all its fullness, of the perfect knowledge which God has of himself, and of creation. The revelation is then complete, perfect and definitive, and in the course of centuries the Church has added nothing to what has been revealed in Christ, but has expressed the content of that revelation in a manner that becomes increasingly explicit and precise. The progress made in the definition of dogmas is not a progress in revelation itself, but in the expression of its content.

Revealed truths are therefore the truth which the human intellect would never have been able to know or discover through its natural capacity, and which it has not by itself any means of proving or verifying. Left to ourselves we are absolutely unable to know whether these are true or false, and we know them only because God has revealed them by his Word. Consequently it is of the utmost importance not to confuse these two domains, absolutely distinct as they are, of scientific and philosophical truths on the one hand and revealed truths on the other. The Church is ever anxious to avoid such confusion, and the distinction has been emphasized by the Council of the Vatican, as also by St Pius X, in his Encyclical *Pascendi*, and Pius XII in *Humani Generis*. All that we know about grace is revealed truth, and we can know nothing about it by natural means.

Our intellect clings to revealed truth by believing what God tells us because he is infinite and perfect Truth, which can neither be deceived nor deceive. It is this adherence which we call faith, and that is why the revealed truths are called "truths of faith" and their exact definition by the Church "articles of faith", or dogmas. As we ourselves have no means of knowing whether the revealed truths are true or false, we can only believe them.

By faith, by understanding and believing what God tells us, we enter into personal relations with him who speaks to us, and are led by him to know what he alone knows in his divine knowledge. That is an all-important fact for the doctrine of grace and will be emphasized further on, when we come to explain the nature of faith and its essentially supernatural character.

Theology is an endeavour of the human intellect to explain revealed truths, not indeed to make us understand or prove them, which would do away with the mystery—since theology shows that, on the contrary, revealed truths are incomprehensible and cannot be proved, and gives us still more the sense of mystery—but to make their meaning precise, to link together the formulas in which the revealed mysteries are expressed and remove all ambiguity. Thus theology assumes the faith that serves it as a foundation and starting-point. The theology of grace is possible only if we believe what God has revealed to us about grace.

The most striking example of the difference between a naturally knowable truth and a truth knowable naturally and revealed truth is incontestably that of the knowledge of God.

We have seen that the human intellect is naturally capable of knowing the Creator indirectly by means of the creatures of which he is the Cause, but what God is in himself, in his divine reality, is an unfathomable mystery for it. Now revelation teaches us and reveals to us what God is in himself: the infinite life of a perfect community of Three Persons, who are the same infinite perfection, without division or sharing, and distinguished only by their relations, the one to the other, that is to say by the very thing that unites them. This is the mystery of the Holy Trinity, the revelation of which is the foundation of all Christianity, but which we can know only by faith; since we can neither prove, verify nor understand it, and our human intellect would never by itself have been able to suspect it. By this revelation of the Holy Trinity God informs us of the intimacy of his divine life, and that is essential if we are to explain the mystery of grace, since we shall see that the life of grace is just life in the society and intimacy of the Three divine Persons. Thereby also we shall understand better that creation is pure, divine generosity, and that God has no need to create because, even though he had created nothing, he is not solitary but Three; neither is he sterile, but within himself infinite and perfect fruitfulness: the Father begetting the Son, and the Father and the Son breathing forth the Holy Spirit. We know that if God creates beings distinct from himself the latter are of necessity imperfect; but now we learn that within himself God is Generation of the Perfect and Gift of the Perfect: the Father generating the Son and the Father and the Son giving the Holy Spirit.

We know that of himself God is perfect Understanding and perfect Love. Revelation will teach us what the life of the intellect is in God. Just as our human intellectual life expresses itself within us by an interior word which we call "thought", so is the perfect knowledge which God has of himself expressed within him in an interior word, or an interior thought which, since St John used it, we call Word, and in which all that God is in his infinite perfection, knowing himself perfectly, is completely uttered or expressed. The Word is so perfect an expression of God that St Paul called it "the image of his substance and the splendour of his glory".

But nothing created could thus perfectly express God or utter all that he is: therefore the Word is not created. We say in the Nicene Creed that he is not made but begotten—*genitum non factum*—but, as St John says, "the Word is God": he is God perfectly expressing God and so, as we say again, "begotten". He is not a creature of God but a Son, for to beget means to engender a being of the same nature as oneself. Thus revelation teaches us that God is Father and Son: that is to say, two persons perfectly distinct, for one can only be a father in relation to a son distinct from oneself, and a son in relation to a father distinct from oneself. And yet, they are not two Gods, for God is One. The Father and the Son are one single God, and so one single and same divine Substance—we say in the Creed that they are *consubstantial.* By all that they are in an absolute manner, Father and Son are identical: they are infinite, divine perfection, without any division or sharing. In consequence, they are distinguished only by the relations whereby they are made relative one to the other: Father with respect to the Son, Son with respect to the Father. The Father is distinguished from the Son only by the fatherhood that makes him relative to the Son, and the Son is distinguished from the Father only by his sonship which renders him relative to the Father.

Revelation also teaches us what the life of love is in God. Just as in us the life of love implies something, as it were, in the nature of a weight that pulls, an energy that carries us along, an attraction that draws us towards the object loved, a giving to that object, and what we call a "spirit"—as when we talk about a "family spirit"—so the perfect love which God has in himself gives within God an interior attraction of God to God, a gift of God to God, which in the New Testament is called the Holy Spirit. The Father perfectly expressing himself in the Son, and the Son perfectly expressing the Father are drawn each to the other by a mutual force or weight, and gift of love. Their mutual love issues in an outburst of joy, a breaking forth of the fire that is the Holy Spirit. But God cannot thus be perfectly given to God and break forth in infinite divine joy by anything created; therefore the Holy Spirit is neither created, made nor produced: he is God. He is God giving God perfectly to God. The Holy Spirit is given or breathed forth from God, and is therefore the Third divine Person, really distinct from the Father and the Son; for he is their Spirit only through his relation to them, and yet he is, with them, one single God: one single and same divine substance. He is consubstantial with them, therefore he is identical with the Father and the Son by all that they possess absolutely—divine and infinite perfection, without division or sharing—and is distinguished from them only by his relation to them.

Each of the Three Persons is God, and God is the Three; therefore each possesses in himself the two others; so that it is a perfect community of infinite life between the Three, each possessing the others, yet distinguished by what they give to one another. That is Trinity in Unity and Unity in Trinity.

Such is the mystery of what God is in his divine reality, but revelation also makes known to us the mystery of his intentions in creating us. It teaches us why he created us, to what he destines us, and thus explains to us the real sense and object of our life. This is the mystery of the supernatural order, or the mystery of grace.

SUPERNATURAL LIFE

We devoted a preliminary chapter to examining our natural capabilities according to our human nature, and we concluded by saying that an infinite gulf yawns between the imperfect creature and the perfect Being, and that the former cannot span it under any circumstances or in any way. By himself man can know his Creator by means of his works and love him because of his gifts, but it is impossible naturally for him to know God directly, "as he is", and to love him for himself. Therefore, it is impossible for man, limited to his natural capacities, to enter into personal relations with God, and to be in the least intimate or familiar with him.

Now we have just learnt that through revelation God speaks to us, and by revealing himself to us enters into personal relations with us; that through faith, listening, believing, receiving into ourselves what he tells and reveals to us about himself, we are in personal relation with him, and know him in himself: that, thanks to the revelation of the Holy Trinity, the Three divine Persons make themselves known to us, enter into personal relation with us, and introduce us into their fellowship and friendship.

Thus we already know that there is in us something infinitely surpassing our human nature, something of which the latter does not admit, which can come to us only through a gift from God and which must therefore be called supernatural. We know also that if through our human nature we are men, we are also and at the same time infinitely more than men, thanks to a mysterious divine gift, grafted upon our nature; and which in order to emphasize that it is a purely gratuitous gift from God, we must call grace. This revelation of the supernatural life, or grace, is the subject of the present work, and we must now first explain precisely what is this supernatural gift that makes of us something infinitely more than mere men, and raises us infinitely above all that human nature can confer upon us. Among the very many passages in the New Testament which reveal to us our supernatural destiny, we shall select as fundamental the one that seems to us the most complete, the richest and the most exact. It is to be found in the first Epistle of St John: "See how the Father has shewn his love towards us; that we should be counted as God's sons, should be his sons."[1]

Here, all of a sudden, we learn the essential reality that decides our destiny, and the sense and object of our life. No longer are we only men, but infinitely more, because we are the children of God. What does this mean? St John does not say that we are creatures or works of God, which is clearly evident and can be found out and proved by reason, but that we are sons or children of God. Now one is called a son or a child who receives the same nature as his father and is, therefore, of the same nature. When a carpenter makes a table, it is his handiwork, but not his child because he does not give it the same nature as his own. When a man begets another man, the latter is not his work but his son, because he has bestowed upon him his own human nature. To say that we are not only works and creatures of God but his children, means that God imparts to us and that we receive from him his own divine nature. That is the essential of what is here revealed to us. The very nature of God is communicated to us. St Peter states explicitly that grace makes us *consortes divinae naturae*, that is to say, "sharers of the divine nature".[2]

St John's words, quoted above, are extraordinarily exact. First he says that we are "counted as" sons of God. That might mean no more than an honorary title, a figure of speech, not expressing any reality, as an artist might speak of his pictures as his "children". In such a case they are not really so, since they do not receive from him his human nature; he is merely using a metaphor, or an image. Therefore St John at once adds precisely that we really are God's sons. The expression "son" or "child" of God expresses something real in us: something affecting the reality of what we are, and that means therefore that we really receive the divine nature.

We are here confronted with something infinitely surpassing

[1] 1 John 3. 1.
[2] 2 Peter 1. 4.

our own human nature, and which we can call without hesitation "supernatural" in the sense of something above our nature; but what revelation has just unveiled to us compels us to give to the word "supernatural" a far wider significance; for by imparting to us the very nature of God grace raises us above the entire created order, real or possible, above all created or creatable nature. For example, we have already pointed out that the hierarchy of creatures includes, above the corporal world and that which is both corporal and spiritual, which is man, created beings that are pure spirits, called in Christian language angels. Now grace raises us infinitely above the nature of the most perfect of the angels, for it is not the angelic nature nor the nature of any other creature, however perfect it may be, but the nature of God himself that we are made to share.

That is why St Thomas Aquinas could say that "the grace of a single man is a higher good than the natural perfection of the whole universe".[3] In the little child, just baptized, there is infinitely more than the perfection and beauty of the whole universe and all the angelic orders: there is the very nature and life of God. Henceforth, "supernatural" takes on a sense synonymous with "divine". Pascal has succeeded in expressing this, in his incomparable language, in a passage of which we have previously quoted only the less important portions: "All bodies, the firmament, the stars, the earth and its realms, are not worth the least of the spirits, for he knows all that and himself also, whereas bodies know nothing. All bodies together and all spirits together, and all that they produce, are not worth the smallest movement of charity, for that belongs to an infinitely higher order. From all bodies together, it is impossible to extract the slightest thought, for that belongs to another order. From all bodies and spirits, it is impossible to obtain a movement of true charity, for that belongs to another, that is, to the supernatural order."

[3] *Summa Theol.* 1a 2ae, q. 113, a. 9.

We must be very careful when giving to the word "supernatural" the sense we have just been using. The word is often used to express something that no creature can carry out alone through its natural powers, and which calls for the intervention of the divine omnipotence, such as a miracle. It is then a question of something that is supernatural in its manner of realization, but in which the effect, produced by divine causality, remains natural as regards its own nature. For instance, the causality of the divine omnipotence is necessary in order to raise the dead to life, for no creature can do so, and in such a case we have a sure proof that God has intervened; but the life that is restored to the corpse is its natural, human life, and therefore something which in its own nature is human, not supernatural. Likewise, the same divine causality was necessary in the case of the multiplication of the loaves, for only God can create, that is, give existence to what does not exist. There again, we have a certain proof that he has intervened; yet the bread thus created was not supernatural in its nature, but only by reason of the divine causation needed for its realization, that is, in the manner whereby it was realized. This is sometimes called "the modal supernatural".

Grace, on the contrary, is not only supernatural, like the miracle, because God is its author, or realizing cause, because only he can give it, but it is supernatural in its own nature, by what it is in itself, for grace is not human or angelic, nor natural from any kind of nature created or creatable. Grace is formally and essentially divine. It is the divine nature itself imparted to man. Therefore, it is sometimes said to be "substantially supernatural", and consequently grace is infinitely superior to the greatest of miracles: just as the son begotten of a man is superior to all the works which the human intellect alone can produce. Hence the word "supernatural" will be used in that sense of the essentially supernatural or divine life of grace, which is the life of God bestowed upon man.

If this be the case, it might be asked what difference there is between "sons" of God as we are, and God the Son, the second Person of the Blessed Trinity, of whom we have spoken earlier and whom the Creed tells us is "the only-begotten Son of the Father".

There are two essential differences, which however are indissolubly linked together one to the other.

1. God the Son is substantially God, consubstantial with the Father, as we have said. There is but one divine substance. We are not substantially one with God, but remain created substances, distinct and infinitely distant from God, dependent upon God for everything that we are, and receiving everything from him. Any theory implying a confusion or an identity of substance between man and God would constitute a serious pantheistic error; and the Church has always condemned formulas tinged with this error; on the other hand they are frequently to be found in many religious or mystical theories of eastern origin and widely held in present-day Europe.

2. God the Son is God by nature. It is his nature to be God and therefore, for him, that is not at all supernatural. Consequently, he is God necessarily and eternally, and he cannot be otherwise. As necessarily as God is eternal, so is he the Father who begets, the Son who is begotten, and the Holy Spirit who is the spiration of the other two. We are not God by nature, but only created human beings, imperfect and limited. That is why grace is something that does not belong of right to our nature, which nothing in us can obtain or demand, and which we cannot procure for ourselves under any circumstances or in any manner. We possess it only because God gives it to us out of his pure generosity. The divine nature, which we have not, and cannot procure for ourselves, is in us only because God, who has it himself, communicates it to us "through grace". God bestows it perfectly freely and in no way is he obliged to give it to us. Had he so

willed, he could perfectly well have created us with our human nature only, without grace, and preserved us in that purely natural order in which we should have been only men. The supernatural has nothing inevitable about it but is entirely the free gift of God; the truly essential and fundamental Christian doctrine is the absolute gratuity of the supernatural. Our nature has no right to grace and were it otherwise there would be no grace, for the idea of something due to us is opposed to the notion of grace. As St Thomas teaches us: "Grace, because it is freely given, excludes the notion of something to which we have a right."[4]

For this reason the Catholic faith is opposed to a whole group of erroneous religious ideas which are becoming increasingly widespread in Europe today, and propose some technique, some ascesis, some method or procedure, through which, by means of his own efforts and powers, man may raise himself to God. We have already said that such is an impossibility, seeing that of himself man is unable to go beyond the limits of his human nature. In the Christian religion, everything comes from the divine initiative. God, in his generosity, gives us what we have not and cannot have through any powers of our own, and that is a free gift which we can only receive.

From this, we see how essential to Christianity is the notion of grace, and how it is even what distinguishes this religion from every other religion or mystical system. Therefore the Church severely condemned the heresy of Baius, which rejected the gratuity of the supernatural, maintaining that as we have a certain natural right to the latter, a certain need of it, that "something" obliges God to give us grace. By corrupting our nature, original sin has taken away this right to grace, but the integrity of human nature before the Fall would have included that right. That is why the Church had to condemn as heretical the proposition of Baius: "The elevation of

[4] *Summa Theol.* 1a 2ae, q. 111, a. 1 ad 2.

human nature so that it should have a share in the divine nature was owing to the integrity of our first condition; and consequently must be called natural and not supernatural." More recently, the Encyclical *Humani Generis* of Pius XII has condemned certain contemporary errors according to which God could not create spiritual beings without giving them grace.

Not only is there nothing in human nature that can claim, still less demand as a right, the supernatural life, but our natural faculties cannot even suspect such a possibility. Our human understanding of itself cannot grasp how the divine nature can be communicated to a creature and, in a sense, be grafted on to that creature's own nature, transforming it as the graft transforms the tree. We know that it is possible only because God has revealed to us that it has been effectively realized, but while knowing that such is the case, we cannot understand the mystery. "No eye has seen, no ear has heard, no human heart conceived, the welcome God has prepared for those who love him."[5] This divine gift is, in a sense, a surprise, such as we could not have expected and in which everything comes to us from the freedom and generosity of the divine initiative. And yet, notwithstanding, there is nothing absurd about it, nothing contrary to our nature, for it cannot be contrary to a created nature that infinite and perfect Goodness, which is the author of that nature's existence, should thus overwhelm it beyond all possible expectation and hope, by giving himself to it.

If it is a serious heresy to deny the gratuitous nature of the supernatural, it is no less serious to confuse the natural and supernatural orders, to fail to recognize that they are distinct, and to consider the supernatural as a kind of development or "flowering" of human nature, so that the supernatural becomes natural: something permitted by nature in her evolution, and which, on a last analysis, is no longer supernatural.

[5] 1 Cor. 2. 9.

These heresies are, however, connected; for if nature requires the supernatural, the latter belongs to its development, and can no longer be distinguished from it; and reciprocally if the supernatural is merely the developing of nature, then the latter can claim it of right. These opinions are widely held today, and destroy what is the essential of Christianity, so that nothing is more urgently needed than that an exact idea of the supernatural should be restored to our contemporaries.

In particular, we find frequently that the spiritual nature of the human soul, and our faculties of intellect and free will, are confused with the supernatural; so that only the animal or sensitive part of man can be said to be "natural", whilst all that is specifically human—the spiritual soul, the intellect and free will—is held to be "supernatural", that is to say, divine. Against these theses we must react strongly by making it clear that a man's spiritual soul, his intellect and his free will, belong to his human nature, that they are natural and human and not at all divine, whereas what is divine in us is the supernatural life of grace alone. Those who hold the contrary are confusing the human and the divine. In no sense are "spiritual" and "supernatural" synonymous, at least so long as "spiritual" means simply what belongs to the human spirit. It does happen that in Christian speech we do use the word "spiritual" in the same sense as "supernatural", but in that case it does not stand for what is derived from the human spirit, but what comes from God the Holy Ghost.

This correct use of terms is indispensable in order to avoid the serious confusion which ends, moreover, in another error very widely held at present, and which is a resuscitation of the old heresies of the Manichees, Cathari and Albigensians, namely, that sin is the resistance of the flesh to the spirit, and that therefore matter, the flesh, animal and sensitive life are evil or the principle of evil, while grace is the spiritualization of man—an evolution of the universe towards the spiritual. All Christian tradition, on the contrary, insists that the principle of evil and sin is to be found in the spirit: in the pride and malice of that spirit whereby it resists or refuses grace, and that grace is the supernaturalizing or deifying of the whole man, and therefore of his spirit as well as his flesh.

We have also mentioned the contemporary error of Immanentism, condemned in the Encyclicals *Pascendi* and *Humani Generis*, of St Pius X and Pius XII respectively. According to this doctrine, God is present in us not only as the author of our existence but also as an object of knowledge, directly knowable by our intellect, so that our natural capacities and supernatural gifts are confounded in this spontaneous knowledge of God that man bears within him. Without understanding them, the Immanentists quote the words of the great Christian mystics, who speak of an experience of God's indwelling in us; but all those Catholic mystics state precisely that such an experience is a pure gift of God, the work of grace, of faith, of charity, of the gifts of the Holy Ghost: that is, is something purely supernatural.

Thanks to the necessary precision which we have been emphasizing, we can now resume and conclude our consideration by saying that whereas God the Son is God by nature, and therefore Son of God by nature, we are not God nor the sons of God by nature, but the *adopted* sons of God. Adoption consists in this: that God adopts us for his children, whereas we are not such by nature, so that he does so freely, and without any obligation to do so. But there is an essential difference between the divine adoption and adoption by man; for if the latter can, indeed, change a child very greatly by means of training yet he cannot reach to that child's innermost being, which remains such as heredity has made it. On the contrary, because God is the author of our very being, adoption by him reaches to the deepest centre of that being, and can therefore really change what we are by rendering us not only nominally and legally, but really children of God. We are not merely "honorary" children but truly such, and that means that we are really deified, really made sharers of the divine nature. It is this real sharing in the very nature of God that is known as "sanctifying grace". We must now define exactly this reality of sanctifying grace which is the result of the divine adoption in us.

SANCTIFYING GRACE

To say that we are not God by nature and substantially is the same as saying that grace, which is nothing else than the divine nature itself imparted to us, is not our substantial nature. Our human nature is our substantial nature, what constitutes us humanly. If men's substance is constituted by human nature and not by grace, it means that grace is a quality, or a property, of which the substance of man is the subject: a quality or property inherent in man's substance, rooted in him, belonging to him, and by which he shares in the nature of God. It is only thus that the reality of grace, while being an incomprehensible mystery, is neither a contradiction nor an absurdity. To say that God gives us grace is to say that the author of our existence realizes in us a quality or property grafted upon our natural being, and transforming it to the point of communicating to us, in and by that superadded supernatural being, the divine nature itself.

Grace thus defined is often somewhat technically called "habitual grace": that means that it is, as says Pius XI in his Encyclical *Casti connubii*, "a permanent and lasting principle of supernatural life". More precisely, it is a quality or property which we possess within us, which is established in us by God in order to remain in us, the effect of which is our supernatural life, that is, the life of God thus possessed by us as a habit. The word "habitual" is derived from the Latin word meaning "to have" or "to possess"; in this sense what is "habitual" is what one has, or possesses, in oneself and of which one may dispose.

More commonly, this "habitual grace" is known as "sanctifying grace", which means that in really imparting to us the same nature as God, it makes us really holy with the sanctity of God which is thus given to us. That is why God could say to us from the time of Moses: "You shall be holy unto me because I, the Lord, am holy",[6] and our Lord could command us, in the Sermon on the Mount, "You are to be perfect, as your heavenly Father is perfect".[7] This holiness, given to us by God, and by which we are like to him, renders us pleasing in his sight. We are adorned, bedecked by him with his own sanctity. Therefore the soul that has received grace sings with the prophet Isaias: "Well may I rejoice in the Lord, well may this heart triumph in my God. The deliverance he sends is like a garment that wraps me about, his mercy like a cloak enfolding me; no bridegroom so proud of garland that crowns him, no bride of the necklace she wears."[8] And to the soul in a state of grace God says: "Fair thou art and graceful, my heart's love."[9]

In the Bible and in the liturgy, the soul in grace is constantly compared mystically to the bride, loving and pleasing in the sight of God, her Bridegroom, who has thus beautified her. But such beauty is not only an ornament but real holiness; what God, who is the source of our being, does in us, he does effectively. Thus the Psalmist can sing of "the great mercies he has shown me"[10]; while our Lord prays the Father to "keep them holy through the truth",[11] and St Paul writes to the Ephesians of "the new self which is created in God's image, justified and sanctified in truth".[12]

It is in the innermost depths of our being that grace deifies and sanctifies us, but this radical, or essential holiness, which is grace itself, bears fruit in holy activities of all kinds. We

[6] Lev. 20. 26.
[7] Matt. 5. 48.
[8] Isaias 61. 10.
[9] Song of Songs 6. 3.
[10] Ps. 65. 16.
[11] John 17. 17.
[12] Ephes. 4. 24.

shall explain later on how grace carries with it faith, charity and all the supernatural virtues. Thus by grace we are rendered capable of performing good works, works that are really divine, of which the source is the grace within us, and so our Lord could say to us: "The task I have appointed you is to go out and bear fruit, fruit which will endure."[13]

Again, writing to the Ephesians, St Paul says that God "created us in Christ Jesus pledged to . . . good actions".[14] The whole mystery of grace is summed up in the same apostle's words: "He has chosen us out, in Christ, before the foundation of the world, to be saints, to be blameless in his sight for love of him; marking us out beforehand (so his will decreed) to be his adopted children through Jesus Christ. Thus he would manifest the splendour of that grace by which he has taken us into his favour in the person of his beloved Son."[15]

We must here be very careful to avoid any misunderstanding in the sense in which the word "grace" is used. It can be employed in a wide sense to express any favour granted by God, and God can grant favours to sinners without thereby making them saints. Notably, we have the frequent use of the word "grace" meaning the gifts which man does not have of himself, and which can come only from God: such as the gift of working miracles, of prophecy, of speaking and understanding unknown tongues; but such gifts do not necessarily make a saint of the person who receives them. They may be granted to sinners who are not sanctified thereby, in order to enable them to carry out a public mission entrusted to them. In theological Latin, such a grace is said to be *gratis data* but not *gratum faciens*, which means that it deserves to be called a grace because it is freely given by God, but not because it makes a man pleasing to him or holy. Sanctifying grace is both *gratis data* and *gratum faciens*. Not only is it a pure gift

[13] John 15. 16.
[14] Ephes. 2. 10.
[15] Ephes. 1. 4–6.

of God freely given, but it makes the recipient really holy, really pleasing to him. To put it another way: this gift of God is the gift of an interior sanctity, that really sanctifies man in his inmost being, and not the gift of accomplishing an exterior work, which would not change the man inwardly. We repeat, therefore, that sanctifying grace is infinitely more than a miracle, a prophecy or a vision.

It is important to be clear about this matter in order to avoid the heresies of Luther and Calvin and a certain number of others following their lead, which have denied the presence in us of a quality bestowed by God that really makes us holy. Either they reduce grace to a juridical title, an attribution of something, like the designation of a man who is making a will; or else it is considered merely as the performance of external works, such as the keeping of a set of rules and commandments. The Council of Trent declared heretical the statement that: "Men are justified either by the imputation of the justice of Christ alone, or through the remission of sins alone, without that grace and charity which is infused in their souls by the Holy Spirit and inheres in them"; and against this heresy it says explicitly:

> Justification is not only the remission of sins but also the sanctification and interior renovation of the man, who willingly accepts grace and the gifts of God, in such wise that an unjust or evil man becomes just, and passes from the enmity to the friendship of God, to become an heir in hope of eternal life. Here are the causes of this justification: its final cause that is, its object, is the glory of God and of Christ, and for us life eternal; its efficient cause is God's mercy, which freely cleanses and sanctifies us[16] by filling us with the promised Holy Spirit, by whom we inherit eternal life[17]; its meritorious cause is the only-begotten and beloved Son of the Father, our Lord Jesus Christ, who when we were yet sinners, at enmity with God[18] merited for us the justice, or the friendship of God, and made

[16] 1 Cor. 6. 11.
[17] Ephes. 1. 13.
[18] Rom. 5. 10.

atonement for us in the sight of the Father through his passion on the cross, by reason of the "exceeding charity" wherewith he loved us. The instrumental cause is the sacrament of baptism, which is the sacrament of faith without which no man can be justified. Finally, the unique, formal cause of this justification is divine justice, not inasmuch as God himself is just but in that he renders us just and so, receiving from him this justice, we are immediately spiritually renewed, and consequently are not only considered and treated as just, but truly merit to be called so and to be really so.

Such are the essential definitions of the Catholic faith with respect to grace. The Church has also condemned as heretical this proposition of Baius: "The justification of the sinner by faith consists formally in the keeping of the commandments: that is, in the righteousness of his works, and not in the grace inherent in the soul whereby a man is adopted by God as his son, and thus renewed and made to share in the divine nature, so that once renewed by the Holy Spirit, he can in consequence live a good life and keep the commandments." Earlier on, Benedict XII had condemned the Arminian heresy in these words: "They claim that the passion of Christ alone, without any other gift of God, making us pleasing in his sight, suffices for the remission of sins, and do not recognize that for the latter we need the grace of God that makes us pleasing to him or justifies us."

Here we have two opposing theses: that which holds that man, remaining a sinner, and doing nothing good, obtains through the Passion of Christ a juridical title which causes him to be treated as though he were just, which he is not, and gives him a right to salvation: and one, on the contrary, that teaches that man ceases to be a sinner and becomes just by means of his good works in keeping God's commandments. So according to the first heresy, salvation comes from Christ who saves, and in the second from our works. The dogmatic definitions just quoted, show that these two heresies are connected and lead one to the other, since both reject the reality in us of what we call sanctifying grace: that is, of a divine sanctity which only God can give us and which cannot come from our works, but by which we are renewed and therefore capable of performing works that are really holy.

This reality of sanctifying grace is a mystery the existence of which we could not know save by faith. It is therefore something which we have no natural means of finding out or verifying, and which we cannot possibly understand. If we could prove that grace exists, that would mean that it was a result of our nature, or that God was obliged to give it to us, and then it would no longer be grace. If we could understand it, it would not be formally divine. It is a widespread misunderstanding to think that grace is something perceptible to the senses, something the presence of which we can be aware of, or experience within us. The Immanentist heresy, already mentioned, and condemned by St Pius X and by Pius XII, attributes to us a consciousness of the presence of grace within us. That is impossible. When we say that grace is essentially divine, and therefore a mystery, it is equivalent to saying that its presence in us can in no manner be perceived or felt. All the writings of all the Catholic mystics tell us clearly that mystical experience is an experience of love which takes place in the darkness of faith, which is rooted in faith and consequently does not allow of any consciousness of grace. When her judges asked St Joan d'Arc whether she were in a state of grace, she replied simply: "If I am not, may God put me in it, and if I am may he preserve me therein", which brings out well how grace comes from the divine initiative only, and not from us, and that we cannot be aware of its presence within us.

Hence it is a very grave mistake to confuse grace with what our contemporaries call "religious feeling", that is, something of which we can be aware or prove. Emphatically, grace does not belong to the order of sensibility or feeling, since it is divine and, *ipso facto*, a mystery of faith. Those who try to feel or experience something, to enjoy sensible consolation, some interior titillation or vibration of natural feeling, or again, to secure some experience which will enable them to verify God's presence within them, have forsaken the way of faith, which consists simply in believing, and in consequence have left the way of supernatural life, which can be lived on no other level than faith. To call "graces", as some people do, what are merely sensible consolations, emotional conditions felt or experienced, is a misuse of Catholic terms. This mistake has often been attributed to Pascal by our contemporaries who failed to understand the sense in which he used the word "heart", which, since the days of Rousseau and the romantics, has stood for emotion or sentiment, but cannot bear that sense in the works of Pascal, who had never read the former. With him, it means what it means in Scripture and in the works of the Fathers of the Church, on which Pascal was brought up; and that sense, founded upon the idea of "inwardness", and depth, means the centre of the soul where God acts by his grace, and whence, as we shall see, charity or love arises. Of course, grace may have certain repercussions in our sensitive natures and feelings, just as it has in our good conduct and our good works, but it is quite mistaken to confuse grace itself with such results, which are merely its effects.

GOD LOVES US

Now that we know what grace is, it remains for us to inquire why God bestows such a gift upon us: why he adopts us by imparting to us his divine nature. But St John's words, with which we began, already supply the answer: "See how the Father has shewn his love towards us; that we should be counted as God's sons, should be his sons."[19]

The revelation of supernatural life is, at the same time, the

[19] 1 John 3. 1.

revelation that God loves us, and the essential message of Christianity is the proclamation to men that God loves them. On Christmas night, the angels announced "Peace to men who are loved by God". The Old Testament had told us the same truth,[20] when by the mouth of Jeremias God had declared: "With unchanging love I love thee, and now in mercy I have drawn thee to myself." But in the Gospel, we hear God the Son speaking of us thus to God the Father: "Thou hast bestowed thy love upon them as thou hast bestowed it upon me", while to us directly he says "It was not you that chose me, it was I that chose you",[21] which St Paul thus explains: "How rich is God in mercy, with what an excess of love he loved us! Our sins had made dead men of us, and he, in giving life to Christ, gave life to us too; it is his grace that has saved you; raised us up too, enthroned us too above the heavens, in Christ Jesus. He would have all future ages see, in that clemency which he shewed us in Christ Jesus, the surpassing richness of his grace."[22]

Grace is a free, divine initiative, and the entire supernatural order proceeds therefrom because it is an initiative of love. There is to be found the first source of the mystery: God so loves us that not only has he created us, that is, given us being, with our human nature and all the perfections of intelligence and freedom which it includes, but he has communicated to us his own divine nature, his own divine life has given us all that he is as God so that we may possess all that he is, that we may possess the absolute, infinite and perfect joy that is himself. He has so loved us as to cause us to live in a complete community of life and love with himself, as children established in perfect intimacy and familiarity with the Father, knowing all about their Father, possessing him, receiving a share of all that he is. Grace being thus a community of life

[20] Jer. 31. 3.
[21] John 17. 23 and 15. 16.
[22] Ephes. 2. 4–7.

between man and God, is an exchange of love between man and God, and the soul in a state of grace, speaking of God as a bridegroom who has chosen it for his bride out of love, can say: "All mine, my true love, and I all his."[23] After the Bible, the liturgy and the mystics will never cease to return to this image of an espousal between God and man. Not only does God give us what we are, but he gives us himself. The Creator is not merely a love which gives, but a Lover who gives himself.

Thus are the divine intentions revealed, and henceforth we know why we have been created. God created us to possess that absolute, infinite and perfect joy that he is himself, and desires only to give himself. We now know the object and meaning of our life: not a human happiness limited to our state as men, but joy that is absolute, infinite, perfect; God himself possessed in his fullness, not the natural perfection of man or the full development of our human nature, or, as is said at the present day, the development of the human person, but the perfection of the child of God, the fullness in us of the divine life, the complete possession of God himself. When, in the Sermon on the Mount, our Lord gave the charter of the whole Christian life, he showed us from the first what we ought to be, what we were made to be, and it is no merely human perfection which he sets before us: "You are to be perfect, as your heavenly Father is perfect." Hence what is in question is a divine perfection, the perfection that is the possession of the life of God within us.

Thus is the mystery of our supernatural destiny revealed. But we are still in the dark as to what is this possession of the divine life, and it remains for us to consider in what this living of God's life given by grace consists for us. We must inquire how the radical and essential holiness which grace establishes in us develops and fructifies in divine life, in divine activities derived from that life. In other words, we have yet

[23] Song of Songs 6. 2.

to know that grace is a power of knowing and loving God and an indwelling in us of the Blessed Trinity.

KNOWLEDGE AND LOVE FROM GRACE

We have said that grace enables us to live the life of God, but we have already explained in what that life consists—perfect knowledge of himself and perfect love of himself. If the perfect Being constitutes impenetrable darkness for the limited intellect of every creature, whether angelic or human, of necessity for himself he is perfectly clear, transparent, luminous. He grasps himself, penetrates himself, comprehends himself, perfectly understands himself. But since that is impossible to any creature, it truly belongs to God: it is what constitutes him in his nature and life as God: to know himself perfectly in all his reality and all his divine perfections. In himself, the perfect Being is the proper object of the divine intellect and is not the object of any created intellect; it belongs to the divine nature by right to be thus for himself the object of a perfect knowledge. Likewise, if the infinite Being is inaccessible to every creature, angelic or human, who can love him only for the gifts of which he is the source, but cannot love him for himself, on the other hand the infinite God, possessing himself perfectly, is necessarily perfect love of himself for his own sake. But since that is impossible to any creature, it is truly proper to God. To love himself thus perfectly for himself, in all his reality and in all his divine perfections, in all his infinite goodness, is what constitutes him in his nature and life as God. The divine Being in himself is the proper object of the divine will and is not the object of any created will, so that it belongs properly to the nature of God to be thus for himself the object of a perfect love.

There we have what properly constitutes the nature and life of God, and it is that which grace imparts to us, giving us the life of God by making us capable of knowing God in himself, in all his divine reality as he knows and loves himself—to know and love him no longer in a human fashion, through the medium of his creatures and because of his gifts, but in a divine manner that grasps him as he is in himself, and thereby to possess in ourselves by knowledge and love, through knowing and loving him, the absolute, infinite and perfect joy that is God, since that joy is constituted by the perfect possession of his infinite perfection in knowledge and in love.

In other words, grace gives to our human intellect as an object of knowledge what is the proper object of the divine intelligence, that is, God himself in all his reality and all his divine perfection; and grace gives to our human wills as an object of love what is the proper object of the divine will, that is, God himself, loved for his own sake in his infinite, divine goodness. Thus it is that grace deifies us, makes us share in what constitutes the very nature of God, and thereby establishes us, through the complete intimacy of knowledge and love, in a fellowship of love with God, whom we know and love in himself and for himself, as children know and love their father.

We have explained how knowledge and love mean the presence of the object known and loved in the subject knowing and loving, which possesses within itself the known and loved object by knowing and loving it. Thus, then, does grace give us what does not belong to our nature, and what our nature cannot procure by itself—the possession of God present within us as the object of knowledge and love. As St Ignatius of Antioch says, we are then "Christ-bearers". St Paul constantly reminds us that we are living temples, within which God lives and dwells by being known and loved therein. If to know is to enrich one's own being from the being of all that one knows one possesses in oneself through knowledge, then grace truly enriches our human being from the divine Being himself possessed by us through our knowing him: it dilates our human being to the infinite measure of the divine Being whom we possess in ourselves through knowledge. God himself is wholly communicated to us in the knowledge that we have of him. If love draws the lover out of himself and his limits, in a movement of self-giving to the loved object, and thus dilates him in the measure of that object, into which he is drawn, grace really dilates our human being in the infinite measure of the divine Being, into whom love carries us out of ourselves and our limits, draws us entirely in a movement of self-giving; God himself takes us wholly into himself in a complete communication of himself in this movement of love.

This is how we can explain the deification of the human being by grace. It is impossible for man to be God substantially, and it is not by our substance but by knowledge and love that the divine nature is imparted to us. Our union with God by grace is not substantial unity, but only in the order of knowledge and love.[24] That is why the supernatural life is possible only in a being endowed with intellect and will. Our human intellect and will are not natural capacities for knowing and loving God, in himself, but because they are capacities for knowing and loving, the former may be communicated supernaturally to them by the grace to know and love God in himself. Grace can be grafted upon our human nature only by taking root in its capacity for knowing and loving. Therefore it neither contradicts nor destroys our nature but, on the contrary, takes and assumes it in its essential capacities for knowing and loving, in order to deify it; and that is why it will make us fruitful in the truly divine activities of knowing and loving. Thus, as Péguy grasped with a poet's intuition, the tree of nature and the tree of grace become one tree—grace grafted upon nature—and yields divine fruits.

[24] In the technical phraseology of theology we say that by grace man cannot be God entitatively, but becomes God intentionally.

We now know what is meant by human life deified by grace —an interior life in which the soul dwells within itself, as in a living temple, with God by knowing and loving him, and thereby possesses in itself, as an object known and loved, God who is absolute, infinite and perfect joy: God attained in all his intimate friendship. It is for this interior life of knowledge and love that we were created. To the question: "Why did God create us?" our contemporaries reply for the most part: "To work in this world in order to transform it", but the catechism answers "to know and love God".

The folly of many whose minds are taken up with outward things and activity! In reality the true life for which we were created is within them, where they possess that treasure, to be known and loved, which is God with whom they are meant to live. "O souls, created for these great things, and called thereto! What are you doing?", cries out St John of the Cross. How is it that the glory of God's grace in us, that is, of God himself, giving himself wholly, does not take up all our attention and all our desire? When the apostles, preoccupied with the restoration of the kingdom of Israel, and as a result with exterior activity in this world, questioned our Lord, he replied: "The kingdom of God is here within you."[25] When the Samaritan woman asks him whether God should be worshipped at Jerusalem, as was done by the Jews, or on Mount Gerizim, as by the Samaritans, he answers that thenceforth men shall adore him "in spirit and in truth", that is, in the centre of their souls, now become a living temple.

Death will separate us from all the good things of this world, and the end of time will do away with everything which external activity for the transformation of the earth will have built up, but our interior life of knowing and loving God will endure for all eternity, and this will constitute the immortal life of the soul. Moreover, no earthly power can reach in us that interior life of intimate union with God,

[25] Luke 17. 21.

which depends only upon grace and can be destroyed only through our own free will, if we yield to mortal sin. Men can imprison us, torture us, kill us, but they cannot deprive us of the infinite glory and perfect joy which we possess within us through knowing and loving God. We may be confined in a prison cell, that separates us from everything human and, especially, from contact with a priest and from all sacraments, but we shall not be alone. We are never alone, for always we possess within us the Three divine Persons who, abiding with us, living in us, are the object of our knowledge and our love, and we exist only to live in their company and intimacy by thus knowing and loving them.

THE INDWELLING OF THE BLESSED TRINITY

Revelation has taught us that the inner life of God is a Trinity of Persons: the generation of the Son by the Father and the giving of the Holy Spirit by the Father and the Son. If grace causes us to live the very life of God, it is because it causes the Father, Son and Holy Spirit to dwell in us. We thus become temples of the Trinity, and in fact, as we have seen, grace establishes us in a personal relation of knowledge and love with the Three divine Persons, in whose company we live as with living persons. It enables us to delight in the Father, the Son and the Holy Spirit, whom we possess within us as the objects of our knowledge and love. "If man has any love for me . . . he will win my Father's love, and we will both come to him, and make our continual abode with him",[26] says our Lord. We are thus introduced into the life of the Trinity, into the inner life of God, who becomes our life so truly that Christ will ask the Father for us: "That they too may be one in us, as thou, Father, art in me, and I in thee."[27] Thus, God is in us, we are in God, and all of us in one an-

[26] John 14. 23.
[27] John 17. 21.

other, as the Father in the Son and the Son in the Father, in the very unity of the divine Trinity which is communicated to us: this divine family, in which we all live of the divine life whereof the Father is the principle, is the end of all creation.

Like everything that is not God himself, grace is the work of the Three divine Persons, but that does not hinder it from establishing us in personal relations with each one of them, by causing them to live in us in their Trinity in their personal relations, introducing us into their own life. Our adoption as children of God communicates to us through grace the sonship which God the Son possesses by nature, so that it is truly in him, assimilated to him, that we are children begotten with him and in him by the Father. The Father begets God the Son necessarily but us freely. He wills to extend to us the sonship of the eternal Son: the eternal love in which that Son is begotten.

Thus we are loved by God with the same love wherewith God the Father and God the Son love and embrace each other eternally, in that "eternal kiss" and mutual gift which is the Holy Spirit. We are begotten in the eternal Son because we are loved in the Holy Spirit. As that Spirit is the bond and mutual gift of Father and Son, so he is the bond and mutual gift of God and his adopted children. We are taken up, assumed into the eternal love that is the Holy Spirit; but whereas God the Son is there necessarily, we are there because God so wills, freely, by election, choice and adoption. More precisely, we are chosen in the eternal love that is the Holy Spirit.

It is this movement of eternal love which, taking us up and carrying us unto himself, communicates to the deepest source of energy of our being our loving response to the infinite love of God, our own gift to God, which is charity, for it is by the Holy Spirit dwelling in us, and not by ourselves, that we are completely surrendered to the divine love, completely given to God. We are given to God in our eternal predestination in the Son in whom we are begotten, and in the Holy Spirit in whom we are chosen; and it is that which grace imparts to us even to the point of enabling us, knowingly and freely, to live thereby interiorly. St Paul tells the Romans: "The love of God has been poured forth in our hearts by the Holy Spirit, whom we have received."[28] The complete and perfect gift, which is eternally mutually communicated between the Father and the Son, is communicated to us by grace.

Grace, therefore, will make us know God there where alone he is perfectly uttered and expressed, in the Word, or the Son, in whom God expresses himself completely and eternally; and it will make us love and receive God there only where he is perfectly loved and given, in the Holy Spirit, in whom he loves himself and gives himself totally and eternally. And then, we carry with us and possess God in such a manner that through charity, loving God for himself by means of God who is within us, we give God to God, and thus the eternal life of the Holy Spirit is accomplished in us. Fr Garrigou-Lagrange says of the elect, who live in the eternal vision of God, "In them the Father begets his Word; in them the Father and the Son breathe forth Love; charity assimilates them to the Holy Spirit, and the beatific vision renders them like to the Word who assimilates them to the Father whose image he is".

GRACE FRUCTIFIES IN KNOWLEDGE OF GOD

We must now state more precisely what is the knowledge and love of God, of which grace is the source.

In the supernatural knowledge of God, there are two very different stages, that possessed in this life and that after death. In this life, so long as the soul gives life to the body

[28] Rom. 5. 5.

and, consequently, knowledge depends upon sensitive life and can do nothing without it, there can be no question of seeing God, who of necessity remains hidden in impenetrable darkness; so that the only possible supernatural knowledge consists in believing what he reveals to us concerning himself, that is in faith.

Hence it is important to explain exactly the nature of faith and its essentially supernatural or divine character. Faith is an act of the intellect, a faculty of knowledge, because it is a matter of knowing what God reveals to us about himself. (We shall know him only by believing what he tells us.) It is the adherence of our intellect to revealed truths, but since we have no means of finding out by ourselves whether these be true or false we can adhere to them only by believing them. Our adherence to truth that can be known naturally, ascertained or verified by experience, either proved or demonstrated by reason, is compelled by the evidence, whether the immediate evidence of experience or the indirect evidence of the conclusion obtained through the medium of the reason that proves it. Since revealed truths have no evidence which can lead our intelligence to adhere to them, such adherence of the intellect must be governed by the will, which moves all our faculties in their acts. Faith is an act of the intellect moved by the will; that is why it is free and can be refused.

The will acts always for a good: here this good is an infinite and divine enrichment, brought to our intellect, through the knowledge of what God alone knows in his divine intellect. The will always acts from a motive; faith can have no other motive than God himself, absolute, infinite and perfect truth, who guarantees for us what he reveals to us. Thus the motive that defines the nature of faith is God himself, not as the Creator such as we can know him naturally, attaining to him indirectly by means of creatures as their existential cause, but in himself, in his divine, infinite truth making himself known to us: that is, such as we cannot know him naturally.

And the object defining the nature of faith, that which we believe, is what God alone knows in his divine intellect and what no creature can know of itself, that is, God himself. God himself is both the motive and the object of faith: the reason why we believe and what we believe, so that faith thus attains to what our nature cannot attain, God in himself.

Therefore, by ourselves we are not capable of exercising faith. It must be given us by God through the Light of God interiorly taking possession of our intellect, of which it—the Light—is the source, in order to make it believe, and by the grace of God taking possession of our will to make it desire the infinite good of revealed and believed truth. Thus, faith is God's work in us. Faith is essentially supernatural or divine; it is a participation, by believing revelation, in the perfect knowledge that God has of himself, and therefore a communion in the life of God.

Faith is hence infinitely beyond the capacities of reason which cannot by itself attain to it, and infinitely more certain than all the certainties of reason, since it rests upon perfect and infinite truth. And yet, for all that, faith can take root in the earth of our human intellect, where God sows it, because it is not contrary to reason, but even conformable to reason, or "reasonable", because there are reasons for believing. There are all the proofs of the divine origin of revelation, prophecies, miracles, sanctity, etc., which demonstrate that this revelation, coming from God, deserves to be believed or ought to be believed. Pascal neatly sums it up in a few words: "Faith is above and not against reason."

The study of apologetics is the study of these grounds of belief. Its conclusion, or end, is not faith itself, which it cannot cause, but the conclusion that the grounds of belief are reasonable. Between this conclusion and faith there is an abyss impassable for human nature, and which can be spanned only through the divine action exercised by God's grace upon the intellect and will of those who do not refuse it. The grounds of belief are not motives of faith, but only what lead us to decide that revelation is worthy of credence. Faith itself has no other motive than the divine truth revealing itself; whence is derived its absolute and infinite certainty, totally independent of the certainty, more or less great and variable, of the reasons for believing.

If apologetics cannot generate faith, they constitute only the preparation of the ground, like the preliminary labour of the farmer before sowing the seed; they can but prepare and clear the way. Like St John the Baptist, they are not the Light, but point out where the Light may be found. Besides, in this preparation apologetics is not only objective, addressing itself to the intellect by suggesting reasons for believing, but also subjective, trying to carry along also the will, removing obstacles arising from pride and from the passions, acting upon the feelings, being supported already by the preparatory working of grace itself in the depths of the soul. The whole work of Pascal brings this out wonderfully. There is pointed out in a few words the whole nature of our apostolic action, which only prepares the way but cannot bestow faith, for the author of the latter is God alone, acting upon the soul from within.

If faith is infinitely above reason, obviously far more is it above feeling or sensibility, which belongs only to the sensitive part of man. Consequently, there is no more deplorable mistake than to confuse faith, as do so many people at the present day, with what they call "religious feeling", and imagine that it consists in experiencing something within ourselves. M. de la Palisse would tell us that faith does not consist in feeling or experiencing, for the simple reason that it consists in believing, and that what we believe is believed only on the condition that it has not been experienced: that it remains unperceived or obscure, just as we have already said that God cannot be experienced. It is true that by taking possession of our whole being, and so of our feeling as of our intellect and will, faith is able to animate from within even our feelings, and thus to produce sensible effects or repercussions which will often be a help to beginners; but it would be a great mistake to confuse these repercussions of grace in our sensitive nature for faith itself, or to make faith depend upon them. Faith no more depends upon feelings than it depends upon the reasons for believing. It depends only upon God, to whom it causes us to cling, in his absolute truth. When everything within us becomes darkness and dryness, faith remains, provided that we do not refuse to believe in God. It even remains purer than ever when it loses all its supports, for then there remains no longer anything within us saving the pure clinging to God that rests upon God himself.

It is highly important to know that until death there is no other knowledge of God in himself to which man can attain excepting that of faith: no way of reaching God himself except that of faith. St John of the Cross has written the last words on this subject, and they ought to be continually re-read. To seek to reach God by any other means is to forsake the supernatural way to him and enter upon one beset with the most dangerous illusions caused by various forms of illuminism. At the present day, it is necessary to put Catholics on their guard against the particularly unhealthy development of a taste for visions, for direct communication with God, and to warn them against seeking a so-called "religious experience" under all sorts of forms: against the craving for something perceptible to the senses. Now, more than ever, do we need to comment and make people meditate upon our Lord's words to the apostle Thomas: "Blessed are they who have not seen and yet have believed."

It should be noted that many today are gravely mistaken about the subject of mystical experience, which they see only as something that can be perceived by the senses, or is apparent in the feelings, whereas all authentic mystics emphasize that such experience takes place only in the "dark night" of both senses and spirit, that as regards all the natural functioning of our sensitive and intellectual faculties it is a matter of death, silence and darkness. It is as though that natural functioning were paralysed, and our faculties no longer working save under the essentially mysterious action of the Holy Spirit in them. Again, it would be a very serious mistake to consider mystical experience as a direct communication with God, outside or beyond the order of faith. On the contrary, all the Christian mystics state that such experience takes place entirely within the domain of faith, that it is a knowledge of God through faith when the cessation of all the natural working of our faculties renders faith purer and more completely attached to God alone, when the silence of the interior "night of the soul" allows the intellect, which is unable any longer to cling to anything but the divine truth revealing itself, to experience God in a movement of the love that is charity carrying the whole being to him under the action of the Holy Spirit. (There may be an interior experience of the being loved through the presence of that loved object in the actual movement of love, whereby the soul is drawn to him, when such love is sufficiently genuine and sufficiently pure.) Thus mystical experience is the darkness of faith transpierced by the love of charity, but it remains still the darkness of faith in which that love lives. It is an experience of love which can take place only in the darkness of faith.

Hence we can lay it down that until death all supernatural knowledge of God consists in faith, and the life of grace which we have described as being life in the fellowship of the Three divine Persons, dwelling in us as in living temples, is the life of faith: life in faith and by faith. It is by faith that we know the Father, Son and Holy Spirit, revealing themselves to us, and that we live in personal relationship with them. The life of grace is a life in the light of faith: a life wherein our thought and our conduct must be ever enlightened and guided by faith in the perspectives of faith.

But the faith that leaves God in darkness can be only a beginning, a sketch, a germ of the supernatural life and not its full development. What then will be that full unfolding after death? Our Lord said to his Father: "Eternal life is knowing thee",[29] and St John tells us that "we shall see him, then, as he is".[30] St Paul says likewise: "we shall see face to face . . . recognize God as he has recognized me."[31]

Just as the grain buried in the earth must burst forth in order that the plant may emerge and expand in the sunshine, so death takes place in order that supernatural life, begun in faith, may reach its full flowering in the eternal vision. Our eternal destiny is now revealed to us. It will be to see God in his full light: to see him as he sees himself. Then by this vision we shall possess the fullness of joy which is God; we shall be fully satisfied. That is why theologians call this vision "the beatific vision". It is also called "eternal life", because its object is outside time. Its object is God, possessing himself in all fullness without any succession or division, in the single moment of divine eternity.

No created idea can express God: we shall see God in the Word in whom he is eternally expressed perfectly; we shall possess in us the Word in whom God will be expressed in us; we shall be taken and assumed into the Word by whom God will express himself in us. Then our assimilation by adoption to the eternal sonship of God the Son will be perfect. Knowing God through God the Son, living in us, we ourselves shall express God by him and in him; the perfect expression of God in the generation of the Word, in whom we are begotten, being then perfectly accomplished in us. No created light can

[29] John 17. 3.
[30] 1 John 3. 2.
[31] 1 Cor. 13. 12.

make us see God. We shall see God in the light that is himself, which will take complete possession of our understanding of which it is the source in order that it may be seen by us. That is what we mean when we sing in the thirty-fifth psalm, "Thy brightness breaks on our eyes like dawn." Our entire being, which issued from that divine Light, will then be so impregnated therewith, seeing everything in it, that the eternal glory of God, the eternal splendour of God will be in us. For that reason, the eternal vision is called also the "Light of Glory". God the Son said to the Father: "And I have given them the privilege which thou gavest to me",[32] and St John of the Cross cries out to us: "O souls, created for such great things!" In the *Introit* of Tuesday after Whitsun, the Church bids us "Take the joy of your glory, giving thanks to God who has called you to his heavenly kingdom".[33] Finally, St Paul, writing to the Romans, sums up thus: "Not that I count these present sufferings as the measure of that glory which is to be revealed in us."[34]

The life of faith and eternal life are not two lives but, like the seed and the plant, two stages of one and the same life: the first in germ the second fully developed. Indeed, St John of the Cross teaches that to believe by faith and see by the beatific vision have one and the same object. In both cases it is God in his divine reality who is known and believed by faith and beheld in the eternal vision. The object known is thus the same, only the manner of attaining it, whether by believing or seeing, is different. Therefore, the life of faith is truly the seed and the beginning of a life made to develop completely in eternal vision, and tends towards this vision as its term. That is why the life of faith is supernatural life in which we already possess God dwelling in us. "Grace is none

[32] John 17. 22.
[33] 4 Esdras 2. 36–7.
[34] Rom. 8. 18.

other than the beginning of glory in us", says St Thomas Aquinas,[35] and St Augustine tells us: "Although on earth, you are in heaven if you love God." That love, springing forth from grace, is charity.

GRACE BEARS FRUIT IN CHARITY

It would be crudely erroneous to confuse charity with that love of God of which we are naturally capable when we love him as our Creator, because of his gifts: because he has given us existence, human nature, intellect and free will. Charity, of which by ourselves we are incapable, and which is the fruit of grace—and therefore supposes that we know God in himself by faith—is not the love of God as our Creator, elicited by all the benefits and perfections of all kinds which he has given us, but the love of God for his own sake, and so purely on account of his own infinite goodness. Charity, which cannot exist without grace and faith, is not the love of creatures for their Creator, but the love of children for their Father, whom they possess in all his intimacy, in all his divine life as God, which is communicated to them. As God himself, in his infinite and divine truth, is the motive and object of faith, and thereby constitutes the supernatural or divine nature of faith, so is God himself, in his infinite and divine goodness, at one and the same time the motive and object of charity: the reason why we love him and the object we love with the love of charity, which is therefore a love essentially supernatural or divine. When we make an act of charity, we do not say "My God, I love you for your gifts: because you have created me and given me intellect and free will", but "My God, I love you because you are infinitely good and worthy of all love", that is, "It is yourself in your infinite goodness whom I love, and I love you for yourself because of that same infinite and divine goodness. I love you because you are God, and that

[35] *Summa Theol.* 2a 2ae, q. 24, a. 3 ad 2.

alone causes my joy and happiness in this world and in eternity to know that you are God. Whatever may happen to me, whether it be happy or unhappy according to the world's point of view, matters little; since I have no other joy or happiness but yourself, who are my God." "It is good for me to cling to my God", we sing in the Psalms. Charity is a sharing in the perfect love which God bears himself and so, as we have said, it is the life of the Holy Spirit in us and the drawing of our whole being in the Spirit by whom and in whom God is given to us and we to God.

Like all spiritual love, charity is an act of our spiritual faculty for loving what is good: that is, it is an act of our will to which God, who is the source of our existence, the origin of our being, gives the charity by moving our will interiorly. That is why charity is free and we can refuse it. Therefore we must not make the mistake of considering it as sensible love, as a feeling and so something connected with our lower nature. The love of charity consists not in feeling that we love God, but in *willing* God, as infinite goodness known by our intellect in faith. We love God by charity when we *will* God. There is no question of feeling that we love God, but of *willing* to love him. True, since grace takes possession of our whole being to transform it divinely, charity may have some repercussion in the senses; it may call forth a love that is perceptible, and these sense effects may help beginners: but never let us confuse the impressions that may be the sensible overflow of charity with charity itself, which is not a sensible impression but independent of all sensible feeling. And if it happens that, to purify our love, God allows us to live in complete aridity so far as sensible feeling is concerned, so that we are no longer aware of anything but indifference, weariness, or even repugnance, but yet we never refuse him anything but persevere in wanting him for himself alone: then it is that our love of charity becomes purer because completely detached from all that is not its single motive: God himself known by faith alone, to whom we cling resting upon him alone.

In the supernatural knowledge of God are to be found two stages, those of faith and of the eternal vision. There is nothing of that as regards love. Charity, which bears away our whole being, in its deepest centre of energy, to God in all his divine reality, is the same whether God remains hidden and believed in only by faith, or whether he is seen in vision. Whether the object be in darkness or in light, true love goes forth to it by a direct movement without deviation, and reaches it in itself. Whether God be for us darkness or light, our manner of knowing him changes but our manner of giving ourselves to him does not. Charity has not the imperfection of faith, but is perfect even in this life. Faith will vanish to give place to sight, hope will be replaced by full possession, love will not cease but will endure for all eternity, bursting forth from the beatific vision as it now does from faith, as St Paul teaches us.[36] Thus does the love of charity establish continuity between the life of grace in this world and the life of eternal glory. By charity, which means God in us and we in God, we already possess heaven, for as St Augustine says in some lines already cited, "Although on earth, you are in heaven if you love God".

Charity, which lives the life of God in itself and for itself, loves the life of God wherever it is to be found: first in God, then in ourselves to whom it is given, and finally in all those to whom also it has been given as to us. Thus charity includes a supernatural love of self. We love ourselves with the love of charity by loving ourselves for the sake of the life of God that is in us, and is our true good, our true end, the real purpose of our life. This supernatural love of self is quite contrary to egoism. The egoist loves himself for his own limits, shutting himself up in himself, denying himself to all that is

[36] See 1 Cor. 13.

not self, and turning his whole attention to himself, as though, so to say, he is twisted or folded back upon himself. By charity we love ourselves in order to yield ourselves to the inflowing of the divine life within us, and thus we subordinate ourselves to God, and turn all our attention to him. To use an expression of contemporary psychology, egoism is "captative", charity is "oblative".

But God calls all souls to live by his divine life, and thus constitutes all in a single divine family, to which he communicates that life. We cannot be sons of God without being brethren of one another: without a community of life wherein we all live by the same life of God which is bestowed upon us all. Moreover, this supernatural brotherhood is the only universal brotherhood among men; for we can be brethren only by being sons of the same father, and human nature founds among men a natural community but not a brotherhood. Therefore charity enables us to love all our brother men for that same life of God which is in them as it is in us: to love them as ourselves, in the most literal sense and measure of the expression, as making one with us in the same divine life that is given to us, and consequently in exactly the same manner as we love ourselves, for the same motive and object: that is, the life of God, loved in our brethren as in us and served in them as in us, because it is the same in them as in us.

St Paul often emphasizes these essential truths known by faith alone and incomprehensible without it. What happens to our brethren, happens to ourselves; we should rejoice in their joys, suffer in their sufferings, help them in all their needs as we help ourselves, because they and we live one single and same divine life, extended and imparted to us all. If we live by the grace of that divine life, we live by the life of each of our neighbours; their life is ours, we live in them and they in us. We are not really living by the life of God unless we live by that life in all our brethren, unless our hearts are as universal as love itself.

There are not two charities: one the love of God and the other the love of our neighbour, but one, single, theological charity, the object of which is the life of God loved in God and in our neighbour. It is a charity which is, at one and the same time, inseparably filial and fraternal, and fraternal because it is filial. No man can love the Father without loving his neighbour to whom the life of the Father has been given. Moreover, St John has pointed out to us that it may be recognized whether or no our charity is genuine from the way in which we serve the life of God in each of our brethren whom a providential encounter makes our neighbour, from the way in which we give ourselves to the brethren in whom he lives.

Hence we should be vastly mistaken were we to confuse fraternal charity with the natural friendship which human nature leads us to bear one to another, or with philanthropy, humanitarianism and benevolence. To love means to love, will, and serve the good of another. Philanthropy leads us to wish and procure for others the various natural good things demanded by human nature. Charity, the object of which is God living in our brethren, makes us wish for and promote in them their true good, that is, the life of God in them, and its development for life eternal. What charity seeks is the salvation and sanctification of our brethren. It loves God for himself, and its neighbour for God's sake, which is the best way of loving him, since by loving him with the same love wherewith God loves him, we are loving him for his *reality*, which is the work of God. It is then, also, in the best sense, loving him for himself, and for his true good which is in God.

Does charity, thus defined, allow us to will for our neighbour and procure for him, the goods of this world? Yes, certainly, in the measure in which those goods minister to the divine life which we will for him. We must feed, clothe, lodge, visit, comfort, counsel and instruct our brethren, in order to do likewise to the life of God that is in them. Our Lord, in describing the last judgement, taught, once and for all, that what we do for each of our brethren we do for God himself, who dwells within them. But in a case where the goods of this world harm the divine life in our brethren and lead them into sin, it is obvious that true charity cannot will them to have such: to act otherwise would be to will their harm. Hence, we must maintain, against certain too-widely held erroneous views, that under no circumstances can charity allow of tolerance or complacency towards sin or false teaching. Charity requires us to hate and fight against both as the greatest evils that can come upon the brethren we love. The more we love sinners and unbelievers—and we ought to love them to the point of giving our lives for them should the necessity arise—the more must we hate and fight against their sin and unbelief.

How far ought we to carry this love of our neighbour? God willed that his life should be a complete gift of self through love: that is what constitutes grace. Therefore, we cannot live by grace, live of that life of God which is a complete giving of itself, unless we also give ourselves utterly to one another, unless we are completely devoted and consecrated to one another, completely at the service of one another.

The life of grace is essentially a sharing and exchange of love, and thus charity is its essential fruit. Having explained what supernatural life is, we must proceed to consider how we can have it, on what condition it can exist in us. We shall see that this condition is precisely the charity which thus constitutes the essence of Christian life, and how thereby that entire life depends upon God's action which, interiorly moving our being at its deepest level, gives us charity.

CHAPTER IV

THE NECESSARY CONDITIONS OF GRACE

NATURAL AND SUPERNATURAL MORALITY

We have seen that it is our intellect that enables us to see the desired good which is the object of all our acts as well as the liberty we have to decide about them in view of the good we desire. Human nature, therefore, includes a natural morality by which our life and our conduct is directed to our own good by our very selves who are responsible for it. Just as human nature involves that natural morality, so supernature, that is grace, grafted upon human nature, should involve a direction of life and conduct, that is, a supernatural morality.

We have shown how, in practice, all direction of life and conduct, that is, all morality, finds its reason for existence in the final end to which our life and all its acts are directed, that is in what we have called the "absolute good" or "last end". That means the good which we will absolutely because it is subordinated to nothing and everything else is subordinated to it. So our natural morality finds the reason for its existence in the natural last end demanded by our human nature, and this is the greatest perfection attainable by man by his natural powers. It includes both the indirect knowledge of God as our Creator, obtained through the medium of created things, and the love of him for his gifts.

Now Revelation has taught us that this natural last end is not the real object of our life, because the end for which God created us is not a human perfection within man's reach, but a divine perfection which he himself gives us through grace: the perfection of a child of God, the perfection of his own divine life which is given to us. It is not a human happiness, adjusted to our human measure, but the complete possession in a life that is eternal, of the absolute, infinite and perfect Joy that is God. Consequently, eternal life constitutes a supernatural last end: a last end because it is the supreme object to which all else must be subordinated and towards which our whole life must be directed. It is supernatural because of ourselves we cannot tend towards it, and by ourselves can do nothing to reach it. Grace alone both enables us to tend thereto and to reach it. The ordering of life in view of life eternal as the result of grace therefore constitutes a supernatural morality.

This morality differs from natural morality, for if the object is changed the direction to take in order to reach it must needs be changed also, just as the gunner alters the sights of his gun when the object aimed at is altered. Supernatural, or Christian, morality infinitely surpasses natural morality because it envisages an infinitely higher end. Firstly, there is a complete change of the means employed. In natural morality it is enough that our human capacities should make the efforts of which we are naturally capable; in the supernatural life, we can do nothing by ourselves to attain an end that is beyond the reach of all natural capacities. Grace alone enables us to act and to succeed. We shall dwell upon this at some length in the present chapter, in order to show that grace alone enables us to behave in a way compatible with the supernatural end we have in view.

Again, the rules to which we must conform ourselves differ also in the two cases since, as we have seen, these rules function in view of the end to which they guide us. It is enough to read the Sermon on the Mount to learn that Christian life consists in the Gospel beatitudes, and thus perceive how far Christian morality transcends natural morality. Our Lord tells those who are obeying the natural moral law that unless their justice surpasses that of the Scribes they cannot enter the Kingdom of God, and goes as far as to curse a fig tree that was not bearing figs "for it was not the season", in order to bring it home to his hearers that natural good works—to bear fruit in the season—were not enough, and that to gain eternal life he required works of which pure natural goodness alone is incapable, as it is for a tree to produce fruit out of season.

We can easily make this clear by examples. Natural morality requires us to practise towards others natural justice, that is to render to every man his due, but we have seen that Christian morality requires that we give ourselves wholly to others from motives of love. When struck upon one cheek, we are to offer the other, when asked to go a mile we are to go two, etc. Natural religion, that is the duties of man towards the Creator, requires us to include in our lives a certain number of acts of worship, such as to say our morning and evening prayers; but our Lord taught us that we must pray always and not faint, and Christian morality calls for continual prayer, since the supernatural life is an interior life of intimate union with God by knowing and loving him, and prayer is nothing else but that interior "gaze" of knowledge and love which must always be turned towards God.

Finally, as a third example, we shall take humility, which means truth in our estimation of ourselves. In natural morality this right consideration of ourselves enables us to recognize that, as regards our natural capacities, we are capable of many things, whereby we may guide ourselves towards our human perfection. In the supernatural order, humility is the basis of everything else, because we must first recognize that by ourselves we can do absolutely nothing, and that everything must be given us by means of the grace which we can receive only by allowing ourselves to be moulded thereby. Here we see the difference between the Christian saints and the heroes of other religions.

Must we now conclude that human life is subject to two moral systems, one natural the other supernatural, and so "divided"? There can be only one last end, and since everything else is subordinate to that, therefore there can be only one moral order. In the light of revelation, we have seen that our true last end, for which God created us, is eternal life; that is, the supernatural last end. Therefore, we have no other moral system than the supernatural or Christian one. Natural morality is only the abstract consideration of what would result—speaking in a conditional sense—from human nature if we had nothing more than that and were not deified by grace.

Has grace, then, abolished natural morality? We have said that grace is grafted upon nature, and transforms it without destroying it. All natural morality is to be found, entire and in no way suppressed, in the supernatural morality which has assumed the former, and absorbed it into itself. In point of fact, our human perfection is no longer our last end. It remains secondary and subordinate to the supernatural last end, for we cannot be perfect as children of God if we are evil as men by failing in what is required by human nature. If a Christian is bound to accomplish infinitely more than the merely natural good works, at the same time he must not leave the latter undone. He must bear fruit out of season, yes, but he must also bear it in season. Therefore, it is grace itself that enables us to practise the natural virtues and practise them divinely.

Natural morality teaches us to live a life in accord with human nature; supernatural morality teaches us to live a life of grace for which our natural human life exists. We must now consider the content of supernatural morality, in order to learn the consequences of grace in us, and we shall see that this supernatural morality consists entirely in charity.

We must study the conditions of the existence of the life of grace in us, and we shall see that that existence is entirely conditioned by charity. We shall thereby understand how, by causing us to act divinely, grace guides us to eternal life.

CHARITY THE CONDITION OF SUPERNATURAL LIFE

We have seen how the right ordering of our life and conduct depends upon the deep-seated energy of the will which determines the interior orientation of our whole being towards its last end, or its absolute good, in a fundamental willing whereby we will our last end absolutely and everything else in view of that. If this last end is God, who is perfect goodness and infinite joy, possessed in himself in all his divine reality, then at the root of the entire moral life is the movement of grace which, acting at the deepest centre of our being, carries our whole will to God himself. This movement is simply the love of God for himself, that is charity. Therefore charity is that fundamental source of energy that actuates and animates the whole spiritual life.

We have also seen that the problem of natural morality is to know what we can and should do in order to live and act as men and achieve our human perfection. It might be thought by analogy that the problem of supernatural morality is to know what we can and should do in order to live the life of grace and attain to its complete development in eternal life. But then the answer would be that we can do nothing for that, and that it is beyond our reach whatever we may do, seeing that it is purely and simply a gift of grace. The life of God in us and its complete development in eternal life is something we can receive only as a pure gift. The problem of orientating our life is then altered, and we can only put it thus: On what condition does God give us his grace, impart to us his divine life? And the answer is simple. God wills only to give it to us. For that, he created us, and he never refuses it to us. Hence he sets no condition; he is infinite love and infinite mercy, who desires only to give himself to all unconditionally. Therefore we shall have that divine life in us provided that we will it. That is, that since we will what we love, with that movement of spiritual love that is the fundamental orientation of the will, we shall have the divine life in us if we love him for what he is in himself, that is, if we have charity. Charity is thus the essential condition of the existence of supernatural life.

God offers us the possession of absolute joy, infinite and perfect as he is in himself. It is for us to cling by love to this God of love, to accept freely, because we love for itself, this gift he makes to us of himself. God is infinite love giving himself totally. Grace is communion and communication and exchange of love between men and God. The reciprocity of love is its very condition of existence. God gives himself to the love that tends towards him. He has said: "Those who are thirsty shall drink—it is my free gift—out of the spring whose water is life."[1] To those who love him, he will say at the judgement: "Come, you that have received a blessing from my Father, take possession of the kingdom which has been prepared for you since the foundation of the world."[2]

But if we do not desire God because we do not love him, he will never force himself upon us. There can be no question of his constraining us to live by his divine life in spite of ourselves, because to live by that life implies a communion of love, an exchange of love that can take place only freely. There can be no love that is not freely given; love cannot be compelled. Because God created us for this exchange of love, his attitude towards us, freely chosen by himself, is to be an appeal of love addressed to our free will, asking us to cling, for love's sake, to his gift of his love, as the bridegroom asking

[1] Apoc. 21. 6.
[2] Matt. 25. 34.

the bride. And we shall see, by the mystery of redemption that, faced by our sins, that is by our refusals, infinite love goes beyond that gift and becomes pardon. Infinite love reveals itself as infinite mercy, and God begs for our love. Consequently, it is quite erroneous, although very common, to picture God as a tyrant, who uses and abuses his omnipotence in order to constrain and compel us to serve him as slaves when, on the contrary, he has chosen just the contrary attitude of appealing for our love alone.

Our Lord did not come on earth in some dazzling manifestation of his infinite power in order to impose himself upon men, but in the helplessness of a little child, exposed to every danger, and completely within our reach so as to be completely accessible to our love. Subsequently he made use of his omnipotence in the service of his love, by working miracles to relieve loving and trusting souls; but when his enemies would have him work a miracle before their eyes, he would decline to compel their adherence to him by means of his almighty power. When the devil suggested he should work miracles he rejected the temptation, and when nailed to the cross for love of us he remained there in the total powerlessness of death.

To refuse to love God, refuse his gift of himself, because we do not and will not love him, is the mortal sin whereby a soul deprives itself of the life of God, whose only desire is to give himself to it. The word "mortal" implies precisely the deprivation of divine life. The infinite, absolute, perfect joy that is God is offered to the soul, and the latter rejects it because it prefers the poor human gratifications that are within our reach: the goods of this world, the pleasures of the senses, the satisfaction that, through pride, men take in themselves and their independence. In such a case, the soul will have what it wishes, for God will not force us. He created us to adhere to him freely; this adherence we can refuse, and he will respect our free will. Then we are devoured by the continuous fever of concupiscence, of passion and of pride, but it is what we have chosen.

It is a widespread but very grave error to think of sin as a breaking of rules. Sin is a refusal of love in opposition to God: the rejection and contempt of the infinite goodness and infinite joy which gives itself to us. Mortal sin lies only in that freely made decision, which destroys charity, which is incompatible with charity, because such a decision involves the refusal of the love of God, the rejection and contempt of God. When, at death, such a free decision is final and irrevocable, without the possibility of repentance, it means that the soul has chosen hell. The lost soul refuses heaven, which is the possession of God, because it does not love him and does not want him; and God respects that freely made choice, because he does not force man to love him: because heaven implies freedom in a love that is reciprocal.

We shall presently consider the relations between grace and free will, but we can see already that grace implies freedom because grace is a mutual exchange of love. There can be no grace that is not freely accepted, and therefore grace and charity are inseparable, and neither can exist without the other. Charity is the fruit of grace which gives it to us, but mortal sin, which destroys charity, destroys grace. It does not necessarily destroy faith, for there can be a refusal of love without a refusal of light, and in such a case a purely intellectual adherence to the divine truth may subsist, but without leading the sinful will to love. Such a faith is called "dead faith". It remains supernatural, that is, a grace, but a grace limited to the intellectual faculty, without transforming and involving the whole being; and because the being is no longer sanctified or deified, it is not sanctifying grace. Thus the existence of supernatural life and the existence of charity are mutually inclusive. At the same time, we have answered the question as to the orientation of our life. It requires nothing else but charity: charity is the whole of Christianity.

CHARITY THE ESSENCE OF THE CHRISTIAN LIFE

If nothing else is required by Christian life except charity, Christian morality is a very simple matter. Nothing is required save to love God for himself and to do everything from the single motive of this love. That is why the Gospel teaches us that the commandment of love is the only commandment, and includes in itself all the others. In fact, all the more or less detailed rules of Christian conduct, which may be included in a treatise of Moral Theology, according to the Gospel and the saints, merely lay down what precisely is required by the love of God by which we must live through all the possible circumstances of our lives.

What are called "precepts" mean what is absolutely necessary in order to abide in that love or not to turn aside from it; the "counsels" express a line of conduct that is still better although without being necessary. These rules exist only by reason of the charity which is their single motive. They are conditioned by charity and are of use only in view of and in the service of charity. Christian moral life, then, is a life of love and has its exigencies as every life has, and is not merely a series of rules to be obeyed. Above all, it is not a series of prohibitions, for it forbids only what is contrary to the love of God and incompatible with the latter, so that it is capable of destroying it. If everything required is of the very nature of love, nothing in it can be arbitrary. It includes no other sanctions than just what we have willed and chosen: the possession of God for those who want him because they love him, and the privation of God for such as have no desire for him because they do not love him.

If included in the Christian religion there is a Christian moral system, because it implies rules that are demanded simply by love, it is not only a moral system but something quite different and much more, for it is fellowship by love with God.

Grace does not make us obey the commandments out of obedience, but under the free impetus of love. It is because a man loves God, and on account of that love, that he freely does what God wills: that he freely conforms himself to the rules called for by that love. A régime of grace is a régime of freedom. What is done from love is not done for the sake of obeying a rule, but freely. Charity renders us quite free, for everything we do under the free interior urging of the love of God will be good because it is done for him. That is why St Augustine can bid us "Love, and do what you will!"

We have explained how because freedom is restricted and imperfect, it needs rules to guide it and keep it from wandering out of the right way. Grace, which imparts to us the divine nature, imparts to us also the perfect freedom that belongs only to God, because from the moment we live by charity and act only under its impulse our freedom is complete.

Moreover, the soul that lives by charity is not content with doing for love everything God wills; it goes beyond the will of God in order to seek, under all circumstances, what God *prefers*. It is not satisfied with keeping the commandments, that is, with doing what is necessary to abide in love, but it yearns to love him more, and, freely and without compulsion, it seeks perfection. Whenever in Christian phraseology we speak of keeping the commandments, we always mean only the indispensable minimum so as not to lose charity; but the soul that lives by charity, for love's sake, and so of its own free will, does much more than what is binding by the commandments. There is no longer any question of merely obeying the Church's commandment to hear Mass every Sunday and receive Holy Communion once a year for a soul that, living to the full a life of love, would not willingly, for anything in the world, miss daily Mass and Communion, because such is interiorly demanded by its love of God. So St Paul constantly repeats that we are no longer under the law but under the rule of love which is freedom. "You serve grace now, not the law."[3]

It is clear that love is more exacting than all the commandments, for it demands the whole self. The soul that stops at keeping the commandments may, when it has observed them all, think that it has done enough. Such a one may think that he is a good man, may be quite content with himself and even think that God ought to be pleased with him. There we recognize the attitude of the pharisee of the Gospel: an attitude shared by so many people of today who consider themselves good and just, are satisfied with themselves, and think that God should be so also, because they are neither thieves nor adulterers, and perhaps even also abstain from meat on Fridays, hear Mass on Sundays, and say a *Pater* and *Ave* night and morning. But to think that one is loving God sufficiently and has no need of loving him more constitutes that lukewarmness which he tells us in the Apocalypse he will vomit out of his mouth. The true lover never thinks he loves enough, and longs to love ever more perfectly, and where God is concerned it is obvious that we shall never love him enough, since he is the infinite good. Such is the meaning of a celebrated passage quoted by St Augustine: "The measure of loving God is to love him without measure."

The soul that lives a life of love will always think that it does not love God enough and, desiring continually to love him more, will thus never be satisfied with itself. There is no degree of charity that would be sufficient and would content it, so that to love him beyond that degree would be, as it were, excessive, or a privileged vocation reserved for a chosen few. It is to the crowd, and so to mankind in general, whether married people or priests, whether in the world or in the cloister, that our Lord, in the Sermon on the Mount, gives the oft-quoted commandment of perfection—to be perfect as our heavenly Father is perfect.

[3] Rom. 6. 14.

The perfection of charity is proposed to all because to the love of God there is no sufficient measure at which we may stop, refusing to go beyond it and love still more. It is true that this perfection is only a term to which to aspire, and it is never necessary to have reached it, since whoever has the smallest degree of charity in him inescapably has grace in him, but to refuse to aim at perfection, and so refuse to make progress, refuse to love God any better in order to stop at a certain degree of love, is lukewarmness. The Gospel condemns those who try to serve two masters, that is, those who do indeed want to give God a part of their lives, while reserving the remainder for the good things of this world, for the gratifications of sense, for human affection, for themselves, because real love allows of no division. God gives himself wholly to us, love would have us belong wholly to God, and that is why love asks more of us than do all the commandments.

So Christian life consists in living by love, it requires that love to be the first mover and inspirer of all our acts. This we shall now consider more precisely by showing how charity is the principle of merit, progress and judgement.

CHARITY THE PRINCIPLE OF MERIT

We have seen how in natural religion by an act that is morally good, upon which we decide freely, thus being responsible for it, from a motive of our true good, we deserve to obtain that real human good, and do so effectively: but once we have learnt from revelation what is our real destiny, we know that it is no longer a matter of making sure of our human, natural perfection, but of the divine life bestowed upon us by grace, and its fullness in the life of eternity. We have just explained that the one condition upon which grace is given to us is that we should adhere freely to this gift of God by means of charity. Hence the act that is supernaturally good and meritorious, by which the life of grace is obtained and by which it can grow in us and lead us to eternal life, is the act in which the motive for which we freely decide is the love of God in himself; in which it is charity which entails the decision and so the act of which the inspiration and motive is charity. Of ourselves, we are incapable of meriting and obtaining grace, its increase, its fullness in eternal life, but through the love which grace gives us we are enabled to obtain all those supernatural good things, that is to merit supernaturally. Acts that are proportioned to our human capacity can obtain and merit only a human and not a divine good. In order to merit and obtain the infinite good that is God, there must be acts that are really divine, but the love that gives us God himself as the object of love makes us carry out acts which, thus inspired by him, loved for himself, are truly divine.

We thus reach the conclusion that supernatural merit consists uniquely in the love which supplies the motive of our decisions, so that it is quite mistaken to see their merit as depending upon the difficulty or the suffering involved by the effort we make or, again, upon what generosity or natural aptitude we can contribute. The merit of our decisions depends upon absolutely nothing except the love of God that inspires our acts. Only that love is worth having and can count supernaturally.

This truth entails very important consequences. The first is that an act of the highest value, naturally speaking, and one that brings into play the highest virtues and aptitudes in the natural order, even an act calling for heroism or genius, an act that is extraordinary and admirable in the eyes of man, but one that is not inspired by charity; an act the motive of which is something else than the love of God, for himself, whatever may be its natural value, counts for nothing in obtaining eternal life. As the *Imitation* clearly puts it: "Without grace, our merits and natural gifts are nothing worth. Arts, riches, strength, beauty, genius, eloquence, are worthless,

Lord, in thine eyes without grace; for the gifts of nature are common to good and to evil men, but grace or charity belongs to the elect."[4]

But it is especially St Paul, in 1 Corinthians 13, who insists upon these fundamental truths of Christianity. It should be constantly read and pondered on. He tells us that to give all we possess to the poor does not avail us supernaturally unless we do so for the love of God and not from some other motive. May our contemporaries therefore cease to confuse charity with philanthropy and learn that the latter may be present in the highest degree and yet be worth nothing supernaturally. To have sufficient courage to deliver one's body to the flames is of no supernatural value if it be done from any other motive —pride, for example—than the love of God. Finally, he adds that even a faith capable of working miracles even to the removing of mountains is worthless without charity—a point upon which lovers of the extraordinary and the marvellous may well meditate.

The second consequence is that, on the other hand, the most ordinary, the commonest and simplest action, performed in the most humdrum of lives, an action that calls for no suffering, effort or natural aptitude, but of which charity is the motive, since it is done for love of God, merits supernaturally and leads the soul to eternal life. Hence supernatural life is in no sense the privilege of a chosen few, or of a caste, but is absolutely within the reach of all without exception, seeing that it requires only that, of our own free will, we correspond to God's initiative of divine love. Such is possible in the most commonplace life, and by means of the lowliest actions accomplished for love of God. It is within the reach not only of those who possess neither genius nor heroism, but even of such as are the most wanting in aptitudes and natural virtues provided that they do not refuse to love God.

Even a human wastrel, one who labours under natural

[4] *Imitation* B. 3, 14–15.

disabilities, can live by grace and attain eternal life, provided that there remains in him the minimum of freedom necessary to cling to God by that interior movement of love which alone counts. Men may judge him severely, if they judge according to his external behaviour, for which perhaps he is not at all responsible, if it be the result of temperament, heredity, bad upbringing, or his unconscious mechanical reactions. God alone sees what is truly free in him, and perhaps that, notwithstanding his seriously deficient external behaviour, may be an interior movement of the will that causes him to choose God for himself, and in such a case that man is living by grace.

In order to live supernaturally and reach eternal life, we do need supernatural aptitudes and virtues; we need grace, and that God can give to those who are, seemingly, the poorest, humanly speaking, but trust in him alone and not in themselves. When St Paul complained of some serious trial, the nature of which we do not know, and begged God to remove it, he received the answer: "My grace is enough for thee."[5]

May our fellow men today remember that grace alone suffices for everything, and that it is always upon it alone that we must count. So much the worse for those who trust in themselves, their efforts, virtues, natural qualities, and count upon anything else whatever save grace alone. The key to the Christian life is to know that of ourselves we can do nothing, and must expect everything from grace. Consequently, it must be thoroughly understood that that life does not consist in outward conformity to a certain number of rules, but in the interior energy of the will, urged on towards God under the action of grace and loving him for his own sake.

At the same time, we understand all the demands and all the simplicity of the Christian life. It demands that absolutely everything in our lives should be done and suffered for the

[5] 2 Cor. 12. 9.

love of God, since all that is not love of him is of no supernatural value. That means that all our thoughts, words and actions at every moment of life and uninterruptedly have no other motive than the love of God for himself.[6] However, it is neither necessary nor possible that at every moment we should be explicitly aware or consciously expressing this motive, provided that it be the motive that effectively controls our voluntary decision: the motive that moves the deepest energies of our will. But at the same time this demand shows us the perfect simplicity of Christian life, since it simply amounts to doing everything, at every moment, for the love of God. That is living by God.

We thus see how spiritual life, perhaps amid the most absorbing occupations, may yet be one of continual prayer: a life of continual loving attention to God. Not that we should be inattentive to the occupations that are our duty during our earthly life, because those occupations are God's will for us.

For love of him, we must give ourselves to them and give them all the attention they require, just as a mother, out of love for her child, gives her attention to what must be done for him, and thus amid all we do our eyes are ever turned to God because we love him. There is no question of our not concerning ourselves with the things of this world or not caring about them, since God wills us to be concerned with them and gives them to us to be cared for. What does matter is that we should concern ourselves with them for love of him, and love them with the same love wherewith he loves them who causes them to exist, who is the author of what they are, of their true reality; and thus through all the realities that are his work our gaze will be ever turned to him through love.

Thus to apply itself to all the acts of life from love of God,

[6] This is fully achieved only in the case of saints. Souls that are still imperfect often act from mixed motives, as for example in the case of imperfect contrition.

our will needs supernatural aptitudes or virtues which adapt it, as it were, to perform everything under the action of charity. If it is true that our natural virtues, acquired by our efforts and formed by training, suffice to direct us towards a human virtue, according to the natural law, but are quite insufficient for the supernatural life, and to direct us to the life that is eternal, we must conclude that in order to act supernaturally our will receives through grace supernatural virtues, supernatural capacities. We know already that grace does bring with it those vital supernatural helps known as the theological virtues, because their object is God himself: God in his infinite truth for faith, God in his infinite mercy for hope, God in his infinite loving-kindness for charity. These constitute the essentials of Christian life because they adapt us to the knowledge and love of God himself.

But the organism of the supernatural life includes also the supernatural moral virtues, which adapt our wills not to God himself but to our conduct, in order to guide it through love to him and to eternal life. These supernatural moral virtues cannot be acquired through our own efforts, but are given us by grace, and proceed from the same actuation of charity that guides us to God through all our activities; they are animated by the charity that constitutes them in their nature as supernatural virtues by giving them their interior impetus towards God loved for his own sake, knitting them into an indissoluble union resulting from its own vitality. So, in the spiritual life, all progress also comes from charity.

CHARITY THE PRINCIPLE OF PROGRESS

If charity is the motive that renders an act supernaturally good, evidently that act will be more or less good according as the charity is more or less intense: according as the act is decided upon with more or less love of God. Hence the difference in the supernatural value of our different acts depends entirely upon the difference in the intensity of the love that inspires them. The most commonplace and ordinary action done with greater charity is worth more than one that is extraordinary, heroic and admirable, but done with less charity. So neither the difficulty, suffering, effort, or talent involved makes any difference in the value of our acts, since that value comes from and consists only in love. Our Lady, cooking and washing at Nazareth, accomplished acts of greater value and merited more than all the most extraordinary, admirable and heroic actions of all human history, because she acted with greater love of God. As St Catherine of Siena says so simply: "You will be rewarded not according to time and workmanship but according to your degree of love."

We see then that the difference in the supernatural value of men is nothing more than the difference in the intensity of their love. He is worth more whose love is the deeper and stronger. What causes us to possess the divine life in greater or less degree? God desires only to give himself and will never set limits to that gift. Therefore we possess the divine life within us according to the degree in which we will to do so: that is, the degree in which we love him is the exact measure of the intensity of the love wherewith we love him. If we do not possess the divine life in a greater degree than we do, it is simply because we do not will to do so, therefore because of the little love with which we will it.

Our degree of grace is measured by our degree of love. Let us say again that, of course, there is no question of the intensity of our love being "felt" or sensibly experienced. Charity is not a feeling and does not depend upon the reaction which it may have on the senses. It does not matter in the least whether we feel more or less sensible love of God. What does matter is the intensity of the love wherewith our will desires God. It is often when we are making progress that we are less aware of our love for God, and the more strongly our will wants him notwithstanding the lack of sensible fervour. Often, indeed, there supervenes a time of trial when the soul is aware of nothing save an indifference or even distaste for the things of God, and then it is that the will, by persevering despite all this in wanting God for himself, and himself alone, is loving him most intensely.

Progress in the spiritual life, therefore, consists only in progress in love. Grace is increased when charity is increased. For a Christian progress means a greater love of God. The obstacles to this progress are venial sin and imperfection. Whereas mortal sin is an act incompatible with charity, and destroys the latter because such sin involves a refusal to love God, venial sin is not such a refusal. It is not incompatible with charity, and therefore it does not destroy it, but it is not in conformity with charity and therefore it prevents it from increasing. Mortal sin may be compared to someone who when out walking turns away from the right road and gives up the idea of reaching his goal, walking in the opposite direction; whereas venial sin is like one who without abandoning the purpose of reaching the goal, nor turning in the opposite direction, interrupts his progress in order to stop and gather flowers or pick up fruit. Imperfection is not a sin at all; it is an act that is supernaturally good, and therefore in conformity with charity, but one whereby a soul gives to God less than he asks, or loves him less than it should. An example would be to hear Mass only on Sundays instead of daily. So doing, such a soul reins in and slows down the progress of its charity. It may be compared to a man who indeed continues to walk towards his destination, but instead of doing so briskly strolls thither slowly and lazily.

We have seen how there is no limit to the growth of charity, since we can never love God enough and are always urged to love him more. That is why the perfection of charity is set before all as the goal whither we must travel without ever stopping. It is within the reach of all, since it is simply a matter of loving God more. Sanctity is simply that perfect charity to which all souls without exception, in the world or the religious life, priests or in the married state, whatever their natural aptitudes, are called; and it is accessible to all because it demands nothing extraordinary or abnormal, requires no special state of life or particular natural talents, but is simply the perfection of love and of self-giving for love's sake, as the Gospel teaches and as St Teresa of Lisieux and Pius XI have so emphatically reminded us. Of course, of ourselves we are incapable of this perfect charity, but so are we also of the least degree of it. In ourselves we are no more capable of achieving salvation than sanctity. In the supernatural order, we receive everything from grace; therefore it is not a matter of counting upon ourselves, efforts, virtues or natural qualities, but of allowing grace to work in us, opening our hearts to it, never being unfaithful to the grace that wills not only to save us but to sanctify us. Provided we allow ourselves to be sanctified by God, he alone will be the author of our holiness as of our salvation, as all the saints have proclaimed.

The supernatural moral virtues play an important part in the early stages of our progress in charity, by enabling us to perform all the duties of life for the love of God. However, they make us advance only slowly because under the action of the grace that has taken possession of them our natural faculties of intellect and will retain their natural manner of functioning, and at their own pace, by means of acts performed successively, one leading to another, with deliberation, hesitation, effort and slowness. For instance, supernatural prudence deliberates, weighing the pros and cons, in order to know which is the better course to take, so as to be guided to eternal life by conforming itself to the demands of love; hence sometimes it hesitates and feels its way. In order that we may advance more quickly and further, and in addition to the activities that are the supernatural moral virtues, whereby we act under the influence of the grace, it gives us also a receptivity whereby we allow ourselves to be led by the action of the Holy Spirit, and follow his leading, and these receptive faculties are called the gifts of the Holy Ghost. Led by these, we no longer advance at our human pace but at God's, who is leading us and to whom we surrender ourselves. For example, by the gift of counsel the requirements of charity are shown to us interiorly by the Holy Spirit, without all the labour of deliberation, and all the hesitation dictated by supernatural prudence. By the gift of fortitude, we easily surmount the difficulties which the supernatural virtue of fortitude would have enabled us to overcome only at the price of strenuous efforts.

Thus, with the gifts of the Holy Ghost the natural manner of acting of our faculties disappears; we do only what the Spirit makes us do and we do it in his own way, and we are thereby plunged into complete mystery, for his leading is indeed incomprehensible to us. For this reason, while the way of the efforts of the supernatural moral virtues is known as the ascetic life, the life lived under the governance of the gifts of the Holy Spirit is called the mystical life. The ascetic life is like a vessel driven by the efforts of the oarsmen, and the mystical life like a sailing ship which advances as the wind carries it along. In prayer, the mystical life is an experience of God by means of the gifts of understanding and wisdom, but, as we have said, an experience wherein, in the "night of the soul", faith "savours" God in a movement of love that carries on the soul to him. This loving contemplation is "night" so far as the senses and intellect are concerned, since the natural functioning of the latter is suspended, but it is the highest form of the life of faith.[7]

[7] Whereas prophecy, visions, locutions, etc., are extraordinary graces, independent of sanctifying grace, loving contemplation in the night of faith, the simple "gaze" of love upon God, when meditation vanishes in the interior silence of the soul in the presence of the God it loves, constitutes the normal "soaring" of sanctifying grace, through the working of the gifts of understanding and wisdom.

ON CHARITY WE SHALL BE JUDGED

If it is charity which assures the existence and progress of the supernatural life, it is also charity which at death assures its definitive achievement and flowering in eternal life.

We have seen that at the moment when the soul leaves the body freedom, which in this life is unstable, becomes stabilized, and the will makes a final, irrevocable decision of which it will never repent, in which it will persevere eternally. It is only in this life that we can lose grace through mortal sin and recover it by repentance. At death the supernatural life is finally acquired or finally lost, according to the free, irrevocable decision which we then make to adhere by love to the gift of God or to refuse him. At death, as always, God, who wills only to give himself to us, offers himself to us unconditionally and never refuses himself. We are free to will to belong to him because we love him, or to refuse him because we do not love him; but it is then a final decision of which we shall never repent, in which we shall persevere eternally. Therefore, the moment of death is the moment of an irrevocable choice between heaven and hell: heaven meaning simply God himself, infinite and perfect Joy, possessed in all his fullness by the eternal vision, and hell, which is simply the privation of God. And the soul chooses which it loves: God, if it loves him, self and its own independence if it loves only self.

So it is charity which, at the moment of death, obtains heaven, or the refusal of charity at the same moment which loses it. Charity is truly the principle of the last judgement. As St Thomas Aquinas and St John of the Cross explain, we are judged upon our love. We must lay aside the childish and human conception of the judgement which represents God as an earthly judge in a court of justice, weighing the evidence for or against the accused. The last judgement means that God, who alone sees to the deepest centre of the soul, discerns the choice which the soul itself makes between heaven and hell, verifies whether or no we have any charity, whither our love is going, and what is our true intention, the real direction in which our will is set.

Thus we see also what a gross caricature of hell is the conception of those who imagine God as a merciless judge, condemning to hell because of their former sins souls who would wish to go to heaven. Not only does God never refuse heaven but, up to the last irrevocable decision at the moment of death, he never ceases to urge us to accept the gift of heaven which is himself. Only those lose heaven who reject it. If at the moment of death someone wants heaven, that is wants God himself, it is because he loves God—for we want what we love—and consequently repents of his former refusals of love, his charity of that moment of death wins God, that is, it gains heaven. Only those are lost who, despite the divine offers and appeals, reject heaven and choose hell. They will not have heaven, which is God, because they do not love him. They are in hell in spite of God, and for ever, because they themselves willed it to be so. They will remain there because henceforth their will is fixed, and cannot change; therefore it perseveres in its rejection of God, and so in refusing the heaven that is God. It perseveres in the proud obduracy that will not surrender to the generosity of love, which will not accept anything because it will not be dependent upon anyone. The lost soul sets all its pleasure in itself: it wills to find everything in itself and to depend only upon itself. Consequently, the lost souls are not in hell despite themselves but voluntarily. They have what they want; but it is what they want that makes their great unhappiness. The case is rather like that encountered in this life of people who obstinately wish for what becomes their misfortune, only with the difference that in this life repentance remains always possible. Lost souls are devoured with rage and despair at the powerlessness of their pride: burnt up in the undying fire of unsatisfied passions, tortured by hatred of God and of one another. Wherever persons live together who are moved solely by pride and passions, feeling only egoistic hatred towards their fellow men, we have an image of hell.

Those who at the hour of death choose God because they love him fall into two categories. If they are not wholly and entirely given to God through love, if their love remains divided between God and themselves, or the good things of this world, they need to be purified in order to enter into eternal life, and that means purgatory. The soul that loves God, yearns for him, and then beholds itself perfectly clearly, suffers from all in it that is not God: all that is an obstacle to its love, and hinders it from seeing and possessing him. This is the cleansing, by means of the devouring fire of suffering love, from all that is opposed to love. This fire of purgatory is therefore the opposite of the fire of hell, which is a fire of suffering through hatred. But because henceforward the will is fixed, love does not increase in purgatory, and that is why it is preferable to do one's purgatory on earth, in the great interior purification through which all the saints have passed in order to become entirely possessed by God. The second category consists of those souls who at the moment of death belong wholly to God, through a love that is undivided. Such as these enter immediately into the eternal joy of their Lord.

One last question remains to be answered. In what degree, or with what intensity, shall we possess eternal joy? Once again, we cannot say, but God desires only to give himself to the soul without reserve. Therefore, we shall possess the eternal joy that is God as fully as we will; that is in the degree in which we love him when death overtakes us. Those who will have less will be those who do not desire him more because of the little love they have borne him. Hence our eternal joy will be in exact proportion to the love wherewith we long for God at the moment of death. The degree of charity a soul has reached at death is the degree of its eternal happiness. The greater glory is for those who love more.

Thus we see now that, from its beginning to its final development, supernatural life depends solely upon charity; but charity of which of ourselves we are incapable is the effect of grace and given us by God. Therefore God is the author of our supernatural life from its beginning to its final consummation. Here the word "grace" bears its full meaning.

GOD THE AUTHOR OF SALVATION AND SANCTIFICATION

We have already quoted St Paul's words to the Romans: The charity of God is poured forth in our hearts by the Holy Spirit whom we have received.[8] Charity is the life of Christ present in us by the Holy Spirit. It is Jesus who, dwelling in us through the gift of the Holy Spirit, loves God perfectly in us through the Holy Spirit by whom we are animated and moved. So St Teresa of Lisieux could write: "When I am charitable, it is only our Lord acting in me." Of ourselves, we are incapable of a single movement of love, unless it comes to us by the grace of Christ abiding in us by the Holy Spirit.

So supernatural life is made real in us through acts inspired by charity, which are truly one act in which we love God with the perfect love wherewith he loves himself: in which, therefore, his whole divine life is communicated to us. But we perform these acts, of which we are incapable by ourselves, only through the action of grace moving us interiorly. By ourselves, we are capable only of natural or human good works, which are of no value for attaining the true object of our life which is life eternal. Our Lord has taught us: "Nobody can come to me without being attracted towards me by the Father",[9] that is, without the grace by which the Father

[8] Rom. 5. 5.
[9] John 6. 44.

adopts us in Jesus Christ as his children. Without that life of Christ engendered in us by the Father we cannot bear any supernatural fruit. Our Lord tells us again: "The branch that does not live on in the vine can yield no fruit of itself; no more can you; if you do not live on in me. I am the vine, you are its branches. If a man lives on in me, and I in him, then he will yield abundant fruit; separated from me, you have no power to do anything."[10] That is why on the third Sunday after Pentecost, the Church prays: "O God, . . . without whom is nothing strong, nothing holy."

St Teresa of Avila has written: "Without grace nothing is possible to us, for of ourselves we cannot think one good thought."[11] The Council of Trent has proclaimed definitively: "As the head over the members and the vine over the branches, Christ Jesus continually exercises his influence upon souls that are justified, and this influence always precedes and accompanies their good acts. Without it, these works can in no way be pleasing to God or meritorious." The same Council condemns as heretical "to say that a man may be rendered just before God by means of the works accomplished, whether by means of his natural and human capabilities, or by keeping the commandments, and without the grace of Christ"; and "to say that without the forestalling action of the Holy Spirit and his help, man can believe, hope, love or repent in the manner that is necessary if he is to obtain grace".

From these quotations it is clear that there exists no merit anterior to grace, of which man would be capable by himself, and by means of which he would obtain grace. A grace that we could deserve and obtain by ourselves would be ours by right, and so would not be a pure gift and therefore not grace. As St Paul tells the Romans: "And if it is due to grace, then it is not due to observance of the law; if it were, grace would

[10] John 15. 4–5.
[11] *Way of Perfection*, c. 29.

be no grace at all."[12] St Thomas Aquinas states clearly: "Grace, inasmuch as it is given us gratuitously, excludes all idea of a debt."[13] Grace which enables us to merit or to be worth anything supernaturally, is a pure gift; so that all our supernatural merits, all that is supernaturally good in us, all our supernatural tending to God, are the working of grace in us. Everything comes from that gratuitous love wherewith God loves us and by which he gives us all things. St Paul writes to the Ephesians:

> How rich God is in mercy, with what an excess of love he loved us! Our sins had made dead men of us, and he, in giving life to Christ, gave life to us too; it is his grace that has saved you; raised us up too, enthroned us too above the heavens, in Christ Jesus. He would have all future ages see, in that clemency which he shewed us in Christ Jesus, the surpassing richness of his grace. Yes, it was grace that saved you, with faith for its instrument; it did not come from yourselves, it was God's gift, not from any actions of yours, or there would be room for pride. No, we are his design; God has created us in Christ Jesus, pledged to such good actions as he has prepared beforehand, to be the employment of our lives.[14]

The same apostle says again: "What powers hast thou, that did not come to thee by gift?"[15] and writing to Titus: "He saved us; and it was not thanks to anything we had done for our own justification. In accordance with his own merciful design he saved us, with the cleansing power which gives new birth, and restores our nature through the Holy Spirit, shed on us in abundant measure through our Saviour, Jesus Christ."[16]

St Augustine speaks likewise: "We have obtained to become the temple of God without any anterior merit having

[12] Rom. 11. 6.
[13] *Summa Theol.* 1a 2ae, q. 111, a. 1 ad 2.
[14] Ephes. 2. 4–10.
[15] 1 Cor. 4. 7.
[16] Titus 3. 5.

given us a right to that grace."[17] St Teresa of Lisieux states: "God does not call those who are worthy but those whom he chooses." Finally, St Catherine of Siena writes: "Lord, if thou dost forestall me by the abundance of thy gifts, it is not for the sake of my merits, but because of thy infinite mercy. I recognize that everything I have received from thee is a free gift, for I find nothing good in myself. I cannot do the smallest good action unless thou dost first give me the necessary light, and unless thou dost kindle in me the fire of thy holy love."

This assertion that grace is absolutely gratuitous, without previous merit on our part, is a fundamental dogma. St Paul is constantly returning to it. "He has chosen us out, in Christ, before the foundation of the world, to be saints, to be blameless in his sight for love of him; marking us out beforehand (so his will decreed) to be his adopted children through Jesus Christ. Thus he would manifest the splendour of that grace by which he takes us into his favour in the person of his beloved Son."[18] "Justification comes to us as a free gift from his grace"[19]; "the effect comes, then, from God's mercy, not from man's will, or man's alacrity."[20] Therefore the Council of Trent has defined that "we are freely justified, because nothing of what precedes justification, whether faith or works, can merit the grace of justification".

We have already pointed out regarding our supernatural destiny that the initiative cannot come from man but must come absolutely from God. The proclamation of Christmas night was not "Peace to men of good will", as though the initiative came from the good will of man, but "Peace to men to whom God wills well"; for all initiative comes from the good and loving will of him who wills man's good, and wills it even to the point of giving himself to men. All Christianity

[17] *Serm.* 252.
[18] Ephes. 1. 4–6.
[19] Rom. 3. 24.
[20] *Ibid.* 9. 16.

is a declaration of the love of God to mankind: a love of which God alone has the initiative. That is what our Lord told us: "It was not you that chose me, it was I that chose you . . . The task I have appointed you is to go out and bear fruit, fruit which will endure."[21]

These basic truths must be reaffirmed against all forms of the Pelagian heresy which, although it ought to have disappeared for good after the Council of Orange, nevertheless reappears in all forms of naturalism, humanism, pragmatism or activism. Pelagianism consists in holding that man, of himself, with his own natural capacities and without grace, can accomplish acts that obtain salvation, or eternal life; acts, therefore, by which he may deserve and obtain grace, so that the latter would be no more than a crown, or a completion, of the work of salvation, granted by God according to man's merits. Man would thus be the chief author of his salvation, and attain to eternal life thanks to the efforts of which he is naturally capable. As for Semi-Pelagianism, it does grant that grace is necessary for achieving salvation, but asserts that its beginning may be the work of man alone, solely through his natural means. These heresies destroy the essential doctrine of Christianity. If our destiny is a supernatural one, that is, infinitely beyond all our natural capacities, and truly divine, from beginning to end we have no means of attaining thereto. Everything is given us by God, including, therefore, the work of grace without which we can do absolutely nothing of any supernatural value. Consequently, faith teaches us that it is by grace alone that we can merit or act in any way supernaturally, that by grace God is acting upon us at the deepest centre of our being, and is the author of our salvation and sanctification.

The same truth was clearly set forth in the Old Testament. "A just God and a saviour, there is none beside me",[22] God

[21] John 15. 16.
[22] Isaias 45. 21 (Douay version).

declared by the mouth of Isaias; and the Psalmist sang: "The Lord is the refuge and defence of the innocent",[23] while in Proverbs it is written that "a kindly man wins the Lord's favour".[24] The Gospels and the writings of St Paul repeat the same truth in every one of the texts that we have quoted, and St John Chrysostom returns to it once more in the words: "In what concerns the matter of our salvation, everything is the gift of God."[25] That is why Pope Zosimus thus defined Catholic teaching: "All good thoughts and all good works, all the efforts and all the virtues whereby since the dawn of faith we have made our way to God, have truly God as their author. We firmly believe that all man's merits are preceded by the grace of him to whom we owe both to begin to will what is good, and to continue to do it. . . . When, then, would it happen that we should not need his help? For all our acts, under all circumstances, for all our thoughts and intentions, we must pray that God may aid and protect us." The Council of Orange defined: "Man can be delivered from his wretchedness only by the divine mercy that precedes him . . . if human nature cannot preserve salvation without the grace it has received, still less can it recover salvation if it has lost it."

Abelard, a precursor of modern naturalism and humanism, was condemned for having maintained the thesis that "free-will of itself is sufficient for something of good", and we have already cited a number of passages from the decrees of the Council of Trent confirming these earlier definitions. The Curé d'Ars sums up the same teaching thus: "It is God who inspires our good actions and does them in us." Fr Grou develops St Paul's thought in the words: "What can we do to save ourselves except what God enables us to do?"[26]

Again, we must emphasize that from start to finish our

[23] Ps. 36. 39.
[24] Prov. 12. 2.
[25] *Serm. II in Coloss.*
[26] *Spiritual Maxims*, m. 2.

salvation and sanctification are the work of grace, as is clear from the passages quoted from Pope Zosimus and the Decrees of the Council of Orange. Therefore the author of the *Imitation* prays: "Lord, I need grace in order to begin what is good, to continue and to achieve it; for otherwise I can do nothing."[27] Catholic teaching has been excellently summed up by Fr Rouquette S.J. (in *Etudes*. July–August 1955): "The Council of Trent has solemnly defined that to enter upon the way of salvation—what we call technically the *initium fidei*—can in no way be merited: that once we have embraced that life deified by sanctifying grace we cannot remain in it through our own strength unless God grants us special assistance throughout our lives: that is, that final perseverance, the coincidence of the state of grace and the last moment of life, cannot be merited."

We cannot merit sanctifying grace by any previous virtuous works, otherwise it would not be a grace. The good dispositions which precede and prepare the way for sanctifying grace are themselves the result of God's action in us, moving our will from within. That is, they are the work of what is called *actual grace*, which means God acting in us to cause us to act at the present moment, in contradistinction to *habitual* or *sanctifying* grace, which is a quality abiding in us. If anyone says that since we consent freely and freely adhere to grace, that consent is surely something that comes from man himself and his natural capacities, that it is not given him by God but that in this case man is autonomous, St Thomas Aquinas answers: "Not to put any obstacle in the way of grace is already the work of grace."[28] It is grace acting at the root of our free will that causes the latter to consent.

We cannot preserve sanctifying grace except God acts in us; that is, we need an actual grace of every moment enabling us to live and behave as sanctifying grace requires us to do,

[27] *Imitation* Bk. 3, c. 55.
[28] *In Hebr*. c. 12, 1. 3.

as we have already seen in our consideration of charity. Still less can we make progress unless God works within us, increasing the grace and love of which he is the fountain head. Finally, we cannot attain to the perfection of grace and charity in this life, that is to holiness, unless God acts in us in order to sanctify us; so that our sanctity is not the result of our natural virtues and efforts, but the work of God.

Final perseverance, that is the final choice of heaven at the moment of death, cannot be merited by what has gone before, but requires the actual action of grace in us at the moment of death: to preserve the grace in us, if we have it, or to enable us to recover it if we have it no longer. What precedes it is only a favourable or unfavourable disposition. For that reason, the greatest sinner can be saved if he accepts grace at the moment of death, notwithstanding the fact that his previous dispositions have been contrary and unfavourable to it. Hence, as we have said, no soul is lost except it refuses and rejects grace at that last moment.

Therefore, by the action of his grace, God is truly the author of conversion, salvation, perseverance, progress and sanctity. So, when asked: "Are you in a state of grace?" St Joan of Arc replied: "If I am not, may God put me therein, if I am may he maintain me in it." And the Church prays: "O God, from whom are holy desires, right resolutions and good works." We must pray that he will bring to fruition in us salvation and holiness, but prayer itself is the work of the grace making us pray. In the Gospel parable, we have the contrast between the publican, who expects nothing of himself and puts all his hope in prayer, and the pharisee, who expects everything from himself and does not think he needs grace.

These fundamental truths imply the teaching of predestination found in so many passages from the writings of St Paul, St Augustine and St Thomas, as also in the definitions of the Council of Trent. If it is God who by grace is the cause of the fulfilment of our supernatural destiny, in consequence his loving, generous will predestines us; we are saved or sanctified because God, who loves us, wills our salvation and our sanctity.

Luther and Calvin saw clearly, as against the Pelagians, that of ourselves we are incapable of any good, any merit: that left to our own strength we are irremediably sinners—fundamental truths expressed by the Church in her Lenten liturgy. But the two so-called reformers asserted these truths only to fall into another and equally serious heresy. They claimed that grace is only a forgiveness and a juridical title to salvation, granted to man though he remains a sinner; so that it does not transform us or render us really good and holy. In connection with sanctifying grace, we explained this erroneous teaching, but we must return to it in connection with actual grace for if the Catholic faith teaches that without grace we cannot merit and perform works that are supernaturally good, at the same time it teaches that grace does enable us to merit and to carry out such works. We really and truly merit, but our merits are the result of the grace in us, and are therefore given us by God. Therefore in the Preface of All Saints (used in some places) the Church prays: "O God, who in crowning their merits dost crown thy own gifts." Grace is not something external to us but something within us, causing us to act supernaturally or divinely. All the texts from Holy Scripture, from tradition and the Magisterium of the Church which have been already cited emphasize that it is grace alone that makes us act aright, and that it really and truly makes us act that way. As our Lord says: "I have chosen you and appointed you (or rendered you such) that you should go and bring forth fruit", St Paul tells us that God chose us in Christ from the beginning of the world, that we might be holy and spotless in his sight, whilst in his treatise on Nature and Grace,

St Augustine writes that God heals us not only to blot out our sins, but also to enable us to sin no more.[29]

The heresies of Luther and Calvin were explicitly condemned by the Council of Trent in passages already quoted, and of which we repeat the principal: "Justification is not only the remission of sins, but also the sanctification and interior renovation of the man who is willing to accept God's grace and gifts; so that from being unjust or evil he may become just." "God justifies us and thus, having received this justice from him, we are spiritually and inwardly renewed and consequently are not merely considered and treated as just, but really deserve to be called so, and are truly just." The same Council condemned as heretical the teaching that: "Men are justified either simply by having the justice of Christ imputed to them, or by the remission of their sins, but without grace and love being infused into their souls by the Holy Spirit." Finally, the condemnation of Baius defined that man, "being renewed by the Holy Spirit, is able in consequence to live a good life".

If grace does not interiorly move our will in order to make us act aright freely, and render us good, just and holy, but is only a pardon, a remission of sin, a juridical title to salvation granted by God to man, while the latter still remains evil and sinful, then God would be acting arbitrarily in granting it to some and denying it to others. It would mean that in advance he chooses some to be saved and others to be damned without man's freedom and responsibility having any part in the matter. This logical consequence Calvin ended by accepting, and thus God appears as the most sadistic of tyrants. The heresiarch taught not only a positive predestination to salvation, to which, according to the Catholic faith, we freely consent, but also a negative predestination, or reprobation, whereby certain souls would be predestined to eternal damnation. According to this heresy, men might will eternal life,

[29] *De natura et gratia*, c. 26, n. 29.

yet be lost because God would deny them grace, so that salvation would be impossible for the "reprobate". As against this monstrous idea, the Catholic faith teaches that God wills all to be saved without exception, and gives to all sufficient graces to be saved, so that only those are lost who wilfully reject those graces, and *ipso facto* eternal life. The Gospel teaches us that the divine Light "enlightens every soul born into the world",[30] and such also is the teaching of St Paul, that God always gives us the strength necessary to resist temptation,[31] that it is God's "will that all men should be saved",[32] and that our Lord is the Saviour of all men.[33] The Council of Trent defined, against Calvin, and Innocent X against Jansenism, that salvation is truly and effectively possible to all.

It is never God who denies grace but the malice and pride of the human will which refuses to accept it. The only complete statement of our supernatural destiny is to echo that of St Prosper: "If certain souls are saved, it is by the free loving-kindness of our Saviour. If certain others are lost, it is through their own fault." We must say at the same time that the salvation of those who are saved comes from God, and that those who are lost are the authors of their own loss. It is in fact the gift of grace that enables us to act supernaturally and deserve eternal life, and therefore our salvation comes from God; but those who are lost are so only because they wilfully refused the grace God never denies; consequently, they are alone the cause of their own loss and God is never the cause of a soul's being lost. "The first cause of the lack of grace comes from us", says St Thomas.[34] Hence it is quite erroneous to put on the same level the domain of *good*, which is reality, positive and existent, of which God, the source of all that is, is the author, and that of *evil*, which is not positive and existent

[30] John 1. 9.
[31] 1 Cor. 10. 13.
[32] 1 Tim. 2. 4.
[33] *Ibid.* 4. 10.
[34] *Summa Theol.* 1a 2ae, q. 112, a. 3 ad 3.

reality but the want, the privation of a good, that is, something purely negative that can be explained only by the deficiency of the creature, of which God is in no sense the source. Therefore, with St Paul, we teach the positive predestination to salvation and reject the negative predestination to eternal loss, upheld by Calvin.

A simile may help the reader to understand what we have just been considering. If a room of which the windows and shutters are open is full of light, we are not the cause of the light, but the sunlight is. If, on the other hand, we draw the shutters, the sun is in no way to be blamed for the resulting darkness; it is we ourselves, who have caused it. In other words, the sunlight produces the brightness, which is a positive reality, and our refusal to use that light causes the darkness, which is only negative and a lack, or privation. Likewise, grace produces the positive reality of salvation and our refusal causes the lack or loss of that grace.

These explanations enable us to learn the truth and do away with all error and absurdity. They do not enable us to understand what we must believe without understanding it, since we are concerned with a mystery that can be known only by faith. In order to understand it, we should have to understand the action of God himself in the depths of our being, his creative action that makes us what we are, and that would mean understanding God himself. We should not forget, indeed, that in the case of positive predestination and salvation, our free consent to grace is itself the work of the grace that is not only "sufficient" but "efficacious", acting interiorly upon our will; whereas, on the contrary, in the case of damnation our refusal is our very own: rejecting the sufficient grace, and opposing God who wills that we be saved. Predestination brings it about that we freely consent to grace and make it efficacious by thus consenting. Hence, sin and eternal loss constitute the only means whereby the soul ceases to depend upon God, receives nothing from him and depends only upon itself; and this is just what the pride of the obstinate sinner, and of the lost soul, desires. Thus we can now grasp and state precisely the relation between grace and free will.

DIVINE GRACE AND HUMAN FREEDOM

The difficulty with which many minds find themselves faced, and which we have already answered partially in our preliminary chapter, concerning the universal causality of God, may be thus expressed: since it is grace, in the sense of God's action in us, that causes us to act supernaturally and to merit, and since God is the author of our good actions and our merits, we are not responsible for them, they do not come from us, and we are not free. Now we have stated that our acts which are supernaturally good and deserving of merit are free and responsible acts: that we freely consent to grace and can effectively refuse it, so that we really do merit and act freely under the action of the grace that makes us act. We are the free and responsible authors of our good and meritorious acts, for all that we are not by ourselves alone capable of them, and can perform them only through grace. Put more precisely, the good and meritorious act is both inseparably the work of our will acting freely, and the work of grace that makes us thus act. Our free consent to grace is itself the work of the efficacious grace that makes us able to consent freely. Against Abelard, who maintained that "free will by itself is sufficient for something good", St Bernard explains in his *De Gratia*: "Grace and free will are equally necessary for salvation; grace to give it and free will to receive it. Therefore, let us not attribute one part of the good work to grace and the other to free will; it is accomplished entirely by the common and inseparable action of both: entirely by grace and entirely by free will."

How then explain this inseparable association, or rather unity, of divine grace and human freedom in the supernaturally good action? How reconcile God's action and the free action of the human will, and explain how neither does away with the other? The difficulty arises from the fact that we know only by means of our own experience, and we have experience only of the action of creatures, and none of God's action. Now, no creature can cause existence; it always acts upon something that exists independently of itself and outside itself, in order to transform the latter. A creature can never be inside the being of another creature. Creatures are exterior to one another and act exteriorly upon one another. Only God can create: can confer existence, and by that he is interior to the being of creatures, since he is the source of that being. In this way, the actions of creatures come wholly, at once and inseparably, from themselves and from the action of God who causes them to exist. We have here a mystery which we can state in all certitude, but which we cannot understand; for to understand the divine action would be to understand God himself.

Human freedom is created, and, as we have seen, that means that it has no existence of itself but exists only by receiving existence from God. Therefore, the creative causality of God, far from suppressing human freedom brings it into existence, gives it being, and causes it to be what it is, namely free. Our free action consists only in receiving being from God. As St Paul tells the Philippians, "The will to do it and the accomplishment of that will are something which God accomplishes in you."[35] And Fr Grou comments: "What can we do to save ourselves except what God gives us power to do?"[36] And the Curé d'Ars says: "It is God who inspires our good works and does them in us." When supernatural action is in question, it is grace that gives us not only to exist according to our human nature, but to exist by partaking of the divine nature, which brings into existence our deified freedom and our supernatural or divine action. It is grace that makes of us beings

[35] Phil. 2. 13.
[36] *Spiritual Maxims*, m. 2.

that act supernaturally or divine. St Paul says exactly: "By God's grace, I am what I am."[37]

So we must not think of the action of grace and that of human free will as being the action of two created beings, that is, as two forces exterior one to the other and adding to each other; for then if all came from one it would mean that the other did nothing and did not exist. For example, when two horses draw a carriage, if all the work is done by one it means that the other is doing nothing. Grace is interior to our free will, as the source of its existence, as what actually makes it exist in a supernatural or deified manner, so that our acts do not proceed partly from our freedom and partly from grace, adding to the freedom and acting upon it exteriorly. They proceed entirely from our free will, which is therefore truly free but, *ipso facto*, they proceed entirely from God's creative action, which causes this freedom to exist according to its proper nature which is to be free; and when supernatural acts are in question they thus proceed wholly from the grace that causes our freedom to exist according to a reality of grace, that is, in a supernatural or deified manner. Our freedom would be suppressed by an action exercised upon it from without, but it is not so by the grace which is within it, at the source of its being, since that is the work of God who causes it to exist.

All this has been put shortly and very well by Fr Rouquette, S.J.:

> In reaffirming, against the strong tendency towards Jansenism, the reality of man's share in the work of his salvation, we should not imagine this human collaboration as an independent source of energy, added to the divine energy, like the combined strength of two horses harnessed together to draw the same vehicle; man and God do not make a pair; freedom and grace are not two additional sources of power. Rather is freedom interior to grace, adheres to it and actively consents to the

[37] 1 Cor. 15. 10.

saving work of grace: freedom is itself the flowering of grace. The fact that we are thus willingly involved in the work of our salvation is essential. Thereby we share in the divine action that saves us; without adding anything to it, we bring it about that this saving action is not external to us; that it is ours and that it is God's, wholly of man and, at the same time, wholly of God. It is true that here we touch upon the primordial mystery and can only sketch the contours without penetrating it. Let us note, however, that this mystery of the "inwardness" of free will to grace and of the existential reality of grace and freedom is only one aspect of a higher and deeper mystery, namely, the first, that of the co-existence of Being and of beings.

If God is the source of our natural being, much more is he the source of our supernatural being. But with this divine source we come into contact only through Jesus Christ our Lord; and this subject must form the next chapter of this work.

CHAPTER V

CHRIST THE ONE SOURCE OF GRACE

SIN AND SALVATION

We have often used the word "salvation" as opposed to "loss", in order to express the securing of grace and finally of eternal life. We have also often spoken of the spiritual life, not in contrast to the state of pure human nature without grace but to a state that is evil and sinful in which man is deprived of grace. The preceding chapters have alluded to the sinful condition which is that of man so long as he is not "saved" by Christ. It is this sinful condition, and this need of "salvation", which must now be explained.

To learn of the first origin of sin, we must go behind the human creation. We have pointed out that above the corporeal universe, to which man, who is both natural and spiritual, belongs, there are creatures who are purely spiritual, pure created spirits called by revelation the angels. Like ourselves, they also were created not for the perfection of their own nature, but for supernatural life: created not only with their purely spiritual angelic nature, but with grace that made them sharers in the nature and life of God. Some clung to that gift of God with all their love, and are definitely established in eternal joy. Others, who are the demons, owing to an attitude of pride, refused that divine grace, that is, they willed to be completely independent. They did not desire to receive anything from anyone, but to have only what they had through themselves, or, which comes to the same thing, they refused out of an attitude of Naturalism, because they set all their happiness in their angelic nature, to such a degree that they willed to have everything thereby, and to have nothing that surpassed it or was not derived from it.

Now, because the freedom of a purely spiritual being is perfectly stable, it cannot change and so is incapable of repentance. The decision of the devils, like our own the moment we die, is final, irrevocable and without the possibility of repentance, and has thus constituted that world of sin called hell; a world of rage and despair, owing to the powerlessness of pride to alter the fact that a creature in all that it is, and even in the nature in which it places its satisfaction, does not exist of itself but depends upon God who causes it to be.

The devils led humanity into sin, and thus subjected it to their hard and cruel tyranny, for by imprisoning the creature in itself and shutting it away from others pride creates a world of hatred. In fact, we learn from our Catholic faith that the whole human family without exception is descended from a single pair, from whom it should have inherited grace but from whom instead it inherited sin, as we are taught by St Paul, the Councils of Orange and of Trent, and the Encyclical *Humani generis*. We have here a basic truth of Christianity, known to us only by faith and which cannot be known otherwise. Hence it is a truth which natural science can neither confirm nor diminish.[1]

Had sin not taken place, Adam and Eve would have transmitted grace to their descendants by way of generation, at the same time as they transmitted human nature. We should have

[1] Paleontology can teach us nothing certain as to the first origin of humanity, since there can be no fossils of a living species until such time as the species becomes very numerous.

been conceived in a state of grace, inheriting grace from our parents, because God had attached grace to human nature in a bond so close that they should have been transmitted together. However, Adam and Eve refused and rejected the supernatural life through the same sin of pride or "naturalism"; that is, the will to be absolutely independent and to set their whole happiness in themselves and in their own nature which we have just explained in the case of the devils.

It is a puerile and ridiculous piece of flippancy, contrary to the Biblical account and the tradition and teaching of the Church, to represent original sin as a sin of the flesh; of sexuality or gluttony, contrary to the spirit. Original sin is a sin of malice or spiritual pride, which refuses grace in order to be completely dependent upon self. Like the demons, Adam and Eve wished "to be as gods", to live in absolute independence, deriving everything from themselves and unable to receive anything from anybody. In the powerlessness of their pride, they desired the single property of God that is incommunicable, namely, to have everything of oneself and nothing from another. Thus they refused to receive from the divine generosity the gift of becoming effectively like God through supernatural life: to receive that communication of his divine nature which God willed to make to them by grace. We must state and insist upon the teaching—against the many widespread errors as regards this subject—that original sin is the revolt of nature against grace, and not the revolt of the flesh against the spirit. The latter is only a consequence of the former. The claim to be independent very quickly extends to the flesh and the senses generally, and thereby destroys the interior hierarchy of human nature, in such wise that men delivered over to pride will also be delivered over to their passions, their anger, their concupiscence, their rapacity.

Through their rejection of supernatural life, Adam and Eve not only deprived themselves of it but, at the same time, deprived likewise all their descendants to whom thenceforth they could transmit only what remained to themselves: a human nature turned away from the supernatural life for which it had been created, and setting all its satisfaction in itself, a nature that instead of opening itself to grace shuts itself up in itself and seeks only self: a nature that is deformed and, in a sense, distorted owing to this falling back upon self: in short, a disordered and sinful human nature.

Henceforth, humanity will be like a stream which, poisoned at its source, remains poisoned throughout its course. It is this disordered and sinful human nature which we inherit from all the human generations that have gone before us, and it does not need much perspicacity to learn that, to the depths of our being, we are compact of self-complacency and self-seeking: that we are continually yielding to hatred, pride, covetousness, and other passions, and thereby engendering all the evils of which human history is one long record. Original sin is not a sin committed by each one of us, and for which each of us is responsible (we are responsible only for freely consenting to its consequences in us) but a sin, or a disorder, affecting our whole human nature itself in its *origin*, and hence called original sin.

Moreover, it must not be imagined that, while despoiling us of grace, original sin leaves us in a state of pure nature, healthy and undamaged, like a man who is naked merely by being stripped of his clothes. The loss of supernatural life has left our nature deeply wounded. God could have created us with our human nature only, and with no other destiny, in which case that human nature, in its pure state and a work of God, would have been good, healthy and rightly ordered. But such a human nature has never existed. God created us for the supernatural life, and a human nature that has rejected the latter finds in itself that serious disequilibrium resulting from pride and self-love which has just been explained. It would mean falling into naturalist error to believe that whatever is simply natural or human is good and healthy like every work of God; for all that is simply natural or human henceforth carries within it that disorder of sin, which is the result of rejecting its supernatural destiny. But in avoiding that mistake we must not fall into the opposite one, that of Luther, which holds that human nature has become bad in itself so as to be incapable of being saved by grace. If sin has deformed or injured our nature, the latter nevertheless remains, despite the underlying sin, a nature which, in itself, as a creation of God, is good, and can therefore be saved by being delivered and cleansed from sin.

It is on the hope of that salvation promised by God to Adam and Eve when repentant, and more or less precisely present in all the religious ideas of mankind, that every human generation will live henceforth. Hence we understand the prevailing use of the word "salvation" to explain the recovery of the grace that has been lost. It is clear, however, that man can do nothing by himself to escape from his sinful condition. Salvation can come from God alone. Infinite love has passed from being a gift to being a pardon, by offering to man the salvation that will rescue him from his sinful state by restoring grace to him.

How would we have imagined the promised saviour announced by God himself? Someone rather like St John the Baptist, a man sanctified by God, preaching repentance from sin; then to those who listened to him sin would have been forgiven and grace restored. But in such a case sin would have been pardoned but not atoned for, and we should have received a lesser grace than the innocence of Adam before the fall. In consequence of sin, a certain loss would have remained. The fact is that if the natural moral fault is finite or limited, because it turns man aside from his finite or limited human end, the sin is of infinite malice, because it despises infinite love that is giving itself to us, and rejects infinite good. Therefore, it cannot be repaired except by an act of love of infinite value, of which no man, be he never so holy, is capable.

But God's infinite love has found what we could never have suspected, and realized—the complete atonement for sin by giving us Jesus Christ as our Saviour.

THE GRACE OF CHRIST

The revelation of the mystery of the Trinity has taught us that in God there is one nature and three persons, really distinct one from the other. From the revelation of the mystery of the Incarnation, we learn that in Jesus Christ there is one single Person and two really distinct natures, the divine and the human. Our Lord is not, like us, a man deified or partaking of the divine nature by grace; he is truly and substantially God. Nor is he only apparently man, but is by nature truly and substantially man, and complete man with human sensitiveness, intellect and will, with a human body and a human soul. (We must not confuse the spiritual human soul of Christ, which animates his body and gives him his human nature, with the divine nature.) Therefore in him there are two natures, which are really distinct, and consequently two intellects, a human and a divine, and two wills, a human and a divine. The two natures, however, although really distinct, belong to one single Person, to a single subject of attribution, to a single "I", who can say with perfect truth "I am God and I am Man". The union of these two, really distinct, natures in a single Person, to whom they both belong, is called the *hypostatic union.* This unique Person is necessarily one of the Three Persons of the Trinity; for there are only the Three to possess substantially the divine nature: to be God by nature and substantially. We know precisely that it is the second of the Three, the divine Person of God the Son, who necessarily and eternally is God, in unity of nature and substance with the Father and the Holy Spirit, and who, by a free decision in time, is, through the Motherhood of Mary, truly and substantially Man. Thus truly God the Son is that Man whom the apostles saw and touched, who was born at Christmas, died on Good Friday, and rose again on Easter Day.

As Christ's human nature belongs to the divine Person of God the Son, as its unique subject of attribution, it follows that in him there is no human personality. What constitutes the human nature of our Lord, as personal and distinct from every other, is the fact that it belongs to the divine Person of God the Son, and that implies that the humanity of Christ is in its order absolutely perfect, not with the infinite perfection that belongs only to God in his divine nature, but with every perfection that the human nature can include in the highest degree.

Christ is, then, perfect Man: the most perfect who has ever existed and will exist, the most intelligent, the most virtuous, the most loving, the strongest, the most beautiful. He is not a superman. He is Man and God in a single Person, in such a way that never can any future evolution of creation and humanity produce anything more perfect than Jesus Christ, and the Christianity issuing from him. Consequently, the Christian religion is not like other religions, a provisional system capable of being surpassed and replaced, but the one and only perfect and definitive religion, established for all eternity. Christ is not the product of some evolution of creation and the human race, but a unique "breaking-in" of God upon his creation, establishing in the evolution of the latter a complete discontinuity. He is by nature Head, Chief, King, Master, Teacher of all mankind for ever and ever. In him are all truth and all authority. He can, therefore, act in the name of all mankind in order to atone for sin and, since the least of his human acts is of infinite value because it is the act of a divine Person, he will make superabundant reparation for sin, and from him, who is God, we shall receive infinitely more than, supposing sin had never been, we should have received from Adam, a man deified. Thus through Christ the infinite love of God will give us not less but more, and the forgiveness will be superior to the original gift.

From Jesus Christ, then, will come all grace henceforth, and he will be for us the one and only source of grace; but we must first clearly understand what is to be understood by "grace" when applied to our Lord himself. In his case, it can be understood in two very different senses, which must not be confused.

Firstly, the gift made to the sacred humanity of belonging to God the Son as its subject of attribution is, in one sense, a "grace", and it is in this sense that, as regards the humanity of Christ, theologians talk about "the grace of hypostatic union". That grace belongs to him only, and can never be imparted to us by any title, since it constitutes precisely his unique, divine personality. It would be a complete misunderstanding to confuse it with the sanctifying grace whereby we partake of the same nature.

Secondly, Christ is perfect Man, not only in the natural but also in the supernatural order. Therefore, his human nature must possess, in the highest degree, all the supernatural perfection which humanity can receive, which means that his human nature possesses the fullness of sanctifying grace; and we must not confuse this sanctifying grace whereby Christ's human nature is made to share in the divine or deified nature, with his divine nature itself, or with the grace of hypostatic union, whereby his human nature belongs to the divine Person of God the Son as to its subject of attribution.

The Gospel teaches the fullness of divine grace in Christ[2] but it must be understood that what is here in question is an absolute plenitude that cannot be surpassed, because in him this plenitude of sanctifying grace flows from the grace of the hypostatic union. A human nature of which the subject is God the Son must necessarily be a human nature fully and perfectly deified. Consequently, in him is to be found the

[2] Luke 2. 40, and John 1. 14.

highest possible supernatural perfection, therefore his human intellect possesses the beatific vision in the highest degree, and that from the first moment of his earthly life. Our Lord never had faith or hope (the highest degree of which is to be found in Mary) and his human will possessed charity in the supreme degree. This infinite and perfect charity of the sacred humanity constitutes the mystery of the Sacred Heart. All the grace found, or ever to be found, in all the angels, all the saints, in the entire Church, exists in a superlative degree in Christ Jesus, for no grace can exist that is not supereminently in him.

Furthermore, his fullness is a "fullness of source", for all the grace that is in the whole Church comes from him. As St John tells us, "We have all received something out of his abundance".[3] Therefore we see the difference between the fullness of the grace of Christ and that of our Lady. Certainly, there is in Mary all the grace that will be subsequently distributed among all the saints and throughout the Church, because our Lord communicated to her all the grace that is in himself, but in Mary that fullness is received, all grace coming to her, as to everyone else, from Christ. Christ is the source of all grace, Mary the channel whereby all the grace flowing from her divine Son will pass into the whole Church. Jesus Christ is the fountain head, in this sense that by his divine nature he is the author of grace, and by his human nature he is the Mediator in whom every grace is given to mankind; so that from him, who is Son of God by nature, comes our adoption as God's children.

He is the Head of the Church, the whole supernatural life of which has its origin in him; Mary is as the neck, by which the life passes to reach all the members. It is in that sense that she is the universal Mediatress of graces, because all mankind is, through her, linked to the sacred humanity of the Son whom she conceived and, therefore, to God the Son,

[3] John 1. 16.

whom she bore in his human nature and for which privilege her free consent at the annunciation was required.

Before developing the consequences of the grace of Christ, we must rapidly indicate how he wrought the mystery of the redemption.

SALVATION BY THE CROSS

We have said that any act whatsoever of our Lord, being of infinite value, would have sufficed to make superabundant atonement for sin. In fact, the "exceeding mercy" of infinite love has gone to the length of accomplishing that reparation through the passion and death of Christ.

When explaining this mystery of the redemption, two points must be considered: first, the greater the suffering offered through love the greater is the love that offers it. We are not here speaking of suffering that is undergone with resignation because there is no alternative: that attitude would be stoicism rather than Christianity. Nor are we speaking of the value of suffering, for suffering in itself is an evil and of no value. We know that its value lies always in the degree of love involved. We have mentioned suffering offered through love, and of the value of the love that offers that suffering.

Secondly, the suffering of the heart of Jesus beneath the burden of the sin to be repaired is infinite, because he knows perfectly and loves with an infinite love the infinite goodness of God which is despised by sin, and so he understands perfectly the infinite malice of sin and holds it in infinite horror. That was the suffering which, before he had received any blow or wound, caused him to enter into an agony such that he sweated blood, simply on account of the interior suffering of his Sacred Heart. We see here how the mystery of sin, which we know only by faith, is something quite different from a natural moral fault: quite different from a violation of laws. Because the infinite love of God himself was carried to the point of that total giving of himself, the sin of rejecting him is the murder of God himself made Man in Jesus Christ. Further, because our Lord is infinite being and infinite life, the Creator of being and of life, he infinitely loves being and life, and has, therefore, an infinite horror of death. Only those do not dread death who do not love being and life. We can form some idea of the horror of death in Christ by thinking how, on Good Friday evening, it could be truly said that God was a corpse.

If we have thoroughly grasped these two preliminary considerations, we shall in consequence be able to state the mystery of the redemption: that is, the infinite sanctity of the infinite act of love whereby, out of love, our Lord offers his sufferings and death. That sanctity, infinitely surpassing the evil of sin, infinitely more pleasing to the Father than sin was displeasing to him, giving God infinitely more love than sin denied to him, was therefore the absolute, and outstanding, triumph of infinite Love over sin that was superabundantly atoned for and finally vanquished.

At the same time, we learn the purpose of all creation, the end for which angels and men were created, and for which all the ages of history have followed one another: it is the infinite sanctity of Christ the redeemer, in whom infinite love, triumphing through infinite mercy, is given with such superabundance. And then, by the mystery of redemption we have the divine answer to that mystery of evil which causes such anguish to all those who are ignorant of the Christian revelation. All evils have come from sin, and God allowed sin to enter the world only that it might be superabundantly repaired, compensated for, and wholly overcome through his infinite mercy in the absolute triumph constituted by the infinite sanctity of Christ the Redeemer. Therefore it is that on Easter night the Church proclaims in her triumphant *Exsultet*: "O truly necessary sin of Adam, which was blotted out by the death of Christ! O happy fault, that merited so great a Redeemer!"

Truly, we need not regret the loss of Adam's innocence before the Fall. How far is it surpassed by the sanctity of Christ, our Saviour! Thanks to the infinite mercy of infinite love the end of sin for us is not loss but a gain, and what a gain! From Jesus Christ we shall receive infinitely more than we would have received from an Adam who had not sinned.

From this truth, two highly important consequences follow:

1. In the cross is an infinite source of grace and holiness, capable of atoning superabundantly for any crime or sin whatever, which is as nothing compared to it, and to change the greatest criminal into a saint, as happened in an instant in the case of the penitent thief at the moment when the redemption was being accomplished, and as happens every day all through the Church's history. Hence, we must never give up hope when faced with any degree of sin or malice. Against Luther, it must be maintained that the immeasurable sanctity of the Cross of Christ, without which we are irremediably sinners, does not leave us sinners by merely giving us a juridical title to salvation, but is really communicated to us so that we may cease to be sinners, and may become truly holy through our Lord and in him.

2. The order of grace will be henceforth an order of mercy, in which the essential of the divine plan is the triumph of love over sin through mercy. Jesus and Mary, the Mother of Mercy and Refuge of sinners, came for the sinners which we all are. St Paul could write: "As our fault was amplified, grace has been more amply bestowed than ever."[4] We are living in this order of redeeming grace, in which infinite love flows over the open void of the spiritual poverty of the publican who, like the penitent thief, cries for mercy, and where nothing is worse than to close a soul to grace through the pride of the

[4] Rom. 5. 20.

pharisee, who does not think he stands in any need of mercy. It is this Christian order of grace which in conclusion we must now explain.

OUR INCORPORATION IN CHRIST

Against all forms of Pelagianism and modern Naturalism, the Catholic faith proclaims that without redemption by the Cross of Christ, man, descended from Adam, is a sinner and that his condition is irremediable. That holds good without any exception, even for Mary who, as a daughter of Adam, was destined to original sin, and who was preserved from it only by the foreseen grace of the redemption coming from the Cross of Christ. We are redeemed by a purifying redemption; she was redeemed by a preserving redemption, proper to the Mother of the Redeemer.

Hence for man, descended from Adam, whether he lived before or after our Lord, whether he knew about him or was ignorant of him, there could be no grace unless it came from the cross. The cross is for Adam's progeny the infinite and superabundant but only source of all grace and sanctity. As St Paul writes to the Romans: "For if by the offence of one many died; much more the grace of God, and the gift by the grace of one man Jesus Christ hath abounded unto many. . . . Therefore, as by the offence of one, unto all men to condemnation: so also by the justice of one, unto all men to justification of life."[5]

Our supernatural destiny cannot be realized except through the grace of Christ being poured out upon us. He told us that himself, in an all-important text already quoted: "The branch that does not live on in the vine can yield no fruit of itself; no more can you, if you do not live on in me. I am the vine, you are its branches; if a man lives on in me, and I in him, then he will yield abundant fruit; separated from me, you have no

[5] Rom. 5. 15–18 (Douay version).

power to do anything."[6] There can be no possible supernatural life for us, save in unity of life with our Lord, who is the fountain of life. Therefore, as the branches on the trunk of the tree, we must be grafted upon him, so as to form with him but one living body, one single plant, living on the one life that flows from him who is the trunk, in order to spread into the branches that we are; or to use St Paul's metaphor, unless we are incorporated in him, so as to form with him but one living body, living of the same life that comes from the Head, who is Christ, and flows into us who are his members. The Church is this single plant, of which he is the trunk and we the branches: that single living body of which he is the Head and we the members. Therefore the Church is the organism of grace the unity of which is that of the life of grace, flowing from Christ and circulating in all. Thus the Christian is a new Christ, a prolongation of the life of Christ in a new humanity, redeemed, sanctified and deified by him, and able to say, again with St Paul: "I am alive, or rather, not I; it is Christ that lives in me."[7]

Of ourselves, we have not, and cannot have, merit, virtue or holiness. It is Jesus Christ, living in us, substituting his life of grace for our natural, sinful life, who is our merit and our sanctity. We are capable of meritorious and holy living only in the measure in which we have renounced the sinful, natural life inherited from Adam, our desires and impulses that are purely sensuous, as also our own opinions and self-will, in order to live henceforth the "Christ-life" that must permeate everything in us. That is what is meant by "renouncing Satan, and all his pomps and works" at Baptism. We may recall the definition of the Council of Trent: "As the Head with respect to the members, and the vine with respect to the branches, so Christ unceasingly exercises his influence over men who are justified. This influence always precedes, accompanies and

[6] John 15. 4–5.
[7] Gal. 2. 20.

follows their good actions, and without it their works are in no way pleasing to God or meritorious." Thus, St Teresa of Lisieux said: "When I am charitable, it is only Jesus acting in me."

We have said that the only object of all creation is the infinite sanctity of Christ, the Redeemer; but it is not him alone, since we are a part of that object, for it is "the whole Christ" of St Paul, the "plenitude of Christ" to use St Augustine's words, Jesus Christ in the complete development of his life in all those who are his members, redeemed, sanctified, deified by him: living in him the very life of God, who is infinite Joy, which he came to give to mankind.

Our incorporation in Christ causes us to belong by participation to the divine Person of God the Son, who imparts to us his divine sonship by rendering us adopted children; and it is for this total gift of himself in Christ and by him, that God created all that is. "God became man in order that man might become God", says St Augustine,[8] and St Thomas states more exactly: "Adoptive sonship is really a shared likeness of the eternal sonship of the Word."[9]

Therefore St John writes that "as many as received him, he gave them power to be made the sons of God",[10] and our Lord himself tells us: "Nobody can come to the Father, except through me,"[11] and to his Father he prays thus: "That they all may be one; that they too may be one in us, as thou, Father, art in me, and I in thee; . . . I have given them the privilege which thou gavest me, that they should all be one, as we are one."[12] The end of creation is the Church, which is this unity in God of the life of God given to all those whom, by the

[8] At the offertory of the Mass, the Church prays "that we may be made partakers of his divinity who vouchsafed to become partaker of our humanity, Jesus Christ, thy Son, our Lord".
[9] *Summa Theol.* 3a, q. 3, a. 8.
[10] John 1. 12 (Douay version).
[11] John 14. 6.
[12] John 17. 21–2.

incarnate Son, the Father has deified. Therefore does St Paul write to the Romans: "All those who from the first were known to him, he has destined from the first to be moulded into the image of his Son, who is thus to become the eldest-born among many brethren."[13] Finally, we may quote once more the great text from the Ephesians: "Marking us out beforehand (so his will decreed) to be his adopted children through Jesus Christ."[14]

In order to give himself to us, God chose a humanity raised by the hypostatic union to be the personal possession of God the Son, and consequently furnished with a fullness of grace which would be poured forth upon all those grafted upon it, so that thereby his divine life, which is infinite joy and love giving itself, may extend to all those who are predestined. This entails the first and unique predestination of Mary, to give birth to God the Son in his human nature, and so bind him to all humanity, in the name of whom she will give her free consent, when asked, to God's eternal plan and, in consequence, to the universal distribution of all graces.

So we exist only for the Kingdom of God, first within ourselves, who must be completely possessed by the life of Christ, and then by us through all that portion of mankind where the life of Christ must be diffused through us and for which we are responsible. Every Christian ought to be an apostle, winning the world for Christ's kingdom. The life of grace consists in making him live in us and, through us, where we live and work. It must be Christ who thinks, speaks and acts through us, so that our thoughts, words and actions may be his and not those of a sinful descendant of Adam, so that those who see our lives may see and find Christ in us. That is what has taken place in the case of the saints who have been wholly possessed by our Lord, while others, who are still divided between him and their fallen nature, hide him beneath the

[13] Rom. 8. 29.
[14] Ephes. 1. 5.

mask of all that still remains sinful in them. Of course, only what in us is holy and Christlike belongs to the Church; all that is still sinful belongs to the world, so that the struggle between the Church and the world goes on in us until that holiness is attained wherein everything belongs to the Church and no longer anything to the world. Thus the countenance of the Church is fully seen only in the saints. Everything belonging to the world, that is, to sinful human nature, taking its pleasure in self and refusing the gift of God, must be rooted out through the triumph of the cross, and won for his kingdom: totally surrendered to the outpouring of the divine life in him. All creation rescued from sin by Christ rises in him, transformed in him, to enter into the glory of the life of God.

It remains for us to know how our incorporation in Christ is brought about.

SACRAMENTAL GRACE

Our Saviour himself instituted the means whereby we are engrafted upon him, incorporated in him, and made to share his life. These are the seven sacraments.

A sacrament is, firstly, a visible sign, a reality perceptible to the senses, which signifies or manifests the invisible mysterious realities of supernatural life. In baptism, for instance, the water that cleanses the body signifies the redeeming grace that cleanses the soul from sin, and the words "In the name of the Father, and of the Son, and of the Holy Ghost" signify the indwelling of the Three divine Persons in the soul of the baptized. Such is the case with all the rites of religion: all signify supernatural realities that God alone can give. Consequently, their effect depends upon the dispositions, the love, of those who receive them: they produce their effects *ex opere operantis*, to use the theological term. But what belongs to the seven sacraments instituted by Christ, however, and to them only, thus distinguishing them absolutely from any other religious rite, is that not only do they signify or represent grace, but they really confer it. They effect what they signify, and that because God alone, who is the author of grace, makes use of the sacraments he has instituted as instruments to produce grace in us. God gives us grace through the instrumentality of the sensible signs themselves, which he has instituted in the sacraments to represent and manifest that grace. Therefore, from the moment we are in the conditions and dispositions required to receive a sacrament validly—that is, so that the sacrament may exist—it is no longer in virtue of our interior dispositions that we receive grace, but independently of our dispositions the sacrament used by God as an instrument acts by itself—as we say, *ex opere operato*—in us to produce the grace. In that case, our dispositions intervene only by causing this sacramental grace to bear more or less fruit in us; so that the reception of the sacrament, which is purely the action of Christ in us, engendering grace, is infinitely more important than our preparation and thanksgiving. To deny that would be "naturalism".

Why has God chosen to give us grace thus through sensible means? Because grace is grafted upon human nature without destroying that nature. We have seen that it is an essential law of human nature that nothing penetrates into the intellect save by means of the senses. We have stressed the point that grace is not perceptible to the senses. How then could we know that we receive it, unless it were conferred upon us through the instrumentality of signs that are perceptible to the senses? Further, as we have seen, the Church is nothing else than the full extension of the life of Christ in all those who, redeemed, sanctified and deified by him, are his members in whom he lives. Therefore, like himself, the Church is both human and divine. It is divine in virtue of what constitutes its formal unity: the grace proceeding from Jesus Christ and deifying all those who belong to him. We have here an invisible reality, known to us only through faith, so that the Church is a mystery only to be known through faith, whence it is called the "mystical Body" of Christ.

But, like him, the Church which he instituted and which was born at Pentecost, is a historical, visible reality, clearly manifested in human history. Its very nature, therefore, calls for visible bonds, whereby its members are attached to its divine Head and to one another, and these bonds are the sacraments. By them we are visibly bound to the historical reality of our Lord who has instituted them, and belong visibly to the Church through which they are transmitted.

We are thus able to have a precise notion of the grace given by means of the sacraments. Sacramental grace is clearly nothing else but sanctifying grace, as previously defined, for that is the grace that our Lord imparts to us through the sacraments. Hence there is no difference in nature between sacramental grace and sanctifying grace received through any other channel than the sacraments. In fact, since original sin, all grace, sacramental or otherwise, can come only from Christ, and is consequently an incorporation in him: an interior and mysterious conformation of our being to him in whose image grace engenders us interiorly. But in the case of non-sacramental grace this incorporation and conformation is purely interior, invisible, and constituting a mystery known by God alone, which nothing manifests visibly. Only God knows those who have or have not charity in them. It belongs to sacramental grace to render this incorporation and conformation to our Lord clearly evident,[15] by establishing between him and us a visible bond, a kind of visible resemblance of the members of the Church to the historic reality of Jesus Christ.

In the case of the priest that goes so far as to make of him, as it were, an actor, playing the part of Christ, and in the case

[15] This visible manifestation may, however, be deceptive if the recipient of the sacrament did not receive it voluntarily and freely, or if he were not in the dispositions requisite for receiving it validly.

of the Eucharist so far as to feed us with the true human body of Christ, and to reproduce his immolation on the cross by the apparently separated species of bread and wine, veiling the realities of his Body and Blood. A child who does not resemble its father is, nevertheless, conformed to him in a certain way through heredity, and is truly his child; but that cannot be seen, whereas it is obvious when the child is like him in appearance.

From what has gone before, it is clear that it is also the property of sacramental grace to give us a place and function in the visible organization of the Church—of a baptized, or visible member of the Church, of one who is confirmed, or a militant Christian, of a priest, a married couple who by the love between husband and wife constitute a cell of the Church's life, destined to propagate her through the birth of new Christians or, as a sick person, a penitent, or finally a guest. Here we see what constitutes sacramental grace. The mystery of non-sacramental grace calls for some final explanation.

NON-SACRAMENTAL GRACE IN THE CASE OF NON-CATHOLICS

If the sacraments are the principal and privileged means whereby God gives us grace, they are not the only means, for his action is not limited by his own ordinances and may work by other means.

Firstly, as regards the increase of grace: if it is wrought in us chiefly through the sacraments, as we have seen already, it can also be increased by our own personal acts of true supernatural charity. Baptized Christians, who have lost grace through mortal sin, can recover it through the sacrament of penance if they have only imperfect contrition, that is, sorrow for sin arising from the fear of finally losing God for ever in hell, but they can recover it without the sacrament of penance if they have perfect contrition, that is if they repent purely from love of God, because sin is an offence against him whom we love for himself. In the case of unbaptized souls, the principal and privileged means of obtaining grace is obviously the sacrament of baptism; but it is clear that if it is impossible for a person to receive baptism the desire of baptism is sufficient, and constitutes an equivalent of the sacrament which we call "baptism of desire", that is non-sacramental baptism.

This baptism of desire is *explicit* in the case of those who have learnt of the existence and function of the sacrament and, consequently, know what they want. But there is an *implicit* baptism of desire in the case of those who have either not been taught or have been badly taught about the sacrament of baptism. Such people do not know what they desire, yet they will to surrender themselves to God, to allow him to have his way with them, and consequently they will implicitly all the means of salvation he may choose, so that they would desire to be baptized if they were properly instructed. St Thomas Aquinas teaches that in every man who has psychologically reached the age of reason, that is every man who can use his free will, there is an action of grace inviting him interiorly to love God for himself, and a response of the free will which either surrenders to grace or refuses it, according as the individual adheres or not to what he knows of God, and the means of salvation instituted by him. For those who are sufficiently instructed and can make use of the sacraments, the latter are the necessary means of salvation, for to refuse them would be to refuse the means God has chosen; but in the case of such as are not sufficiently instructed, or cannot possibly obtain the sacraments, God will give grace by other means to whoever does not wilfully reject it.

So, as we have said, grace is truly offered to all. Salvation is possible for all, non-Christians included, who, uninstructed or wrongly instructed concerning the Christian revelation, have not been able to reject it out of malice. This is clear from St John's words, telling us that the Word of God "enlightens every soul born into this world",[16] and St Paul, who declares that God wills that all men should be saved, and that Christ is the Saviour of all.[17] For that reason, Alexander VIII condemned Jansenius, who maintained that pagans, Jews, heretics and others received no influence of Jesus Christ, and the Church declared heretical the teaching of Quesnel that "no grace is given outside the Church", meaning beyond the visible frontiers of the Church, or her visible membership.

So there are two ways of belonging to Christ and to the Church: by visible membership through the sacraments and, for those who lack sufficient knowledge, an invisible membership by means of interior fidelity to the grace that works in every man, and to what he knows of God and the ways of salvation instituted by him. This Catholic thesis of invisible membership of the one visible Church founded by Christ and ruled by the pope and the bishops has nothing to do with the heretical theory of a Church that is purely spiritual and invisible. Those who do not know Christ but do not reject God are saved and sanctified by the one and only source of grace, which is Christ; and by the redeeming grace of him who lives in them they belong invisibly, and without knowing it themselves, to the divine society which he founded as the development and prolongation of his life, the visible Church. Many of our contemporaries are anxious to understand the modality of this membership, but that is impossible just because the membership is invisible. That means that it constitutes a mystery known to God alone, who sees to the uttermost depths of souls, and knows how they respond to his love.

The chief difficulty in the case of non-Christians arises from the fact that grace cannot exist without faith: that is, unless the intellect adheres to the divine truth which reveals the gift of God and salvation. It is clear that the knowledge of God

[16] John 1. 9.
[17] 1 Tim. 2. 4. and 4. 10.

the Creator, derived from the evidence of his visible works—a knowledge possible to all who have the normal use of reason—cannot suffice for a supernatural life of personal intimacy with God. God must be known as the author of salvation, and the intimate friend of our souls, and this knowledge can be had only by revelation. Some writers have proposed the hypothesis of a revelation given by God at the moment of death to all who do not refuse the light; but this hypothesis is insufficient, for it would explain only how grace is received at the actual moment of death, whereas we must admit, with St Thomas Aquinas, that from the age of reason grace is offered by God to non-Christians who have not rejected the truth out of malice, and that their good acts are authentically supernatural and, therefore, enlightened by faith.

There is one case in which the solution of the problem is clear and given by tradition, namely, that of the righteous of the Old Testament, who clung by faith to the promise of the Saviour, and this solution does not apply only to the Jews since among such righteous souls must be numbered Noah, Job and Melchisedech. This leads us to think that, previous to the revelation to the patriarchs and prophets, we must take account of a first revelation of the promise of a Saviour, made to Adam and Eve when repentant, and so at the beginning of human history; and it seems to us that, even amidst the errors and superstition, it is possible to find distorted vestiges of that primitive revelation in all the religious traditions of the human race. Everywhere, there is to be found the expectation of a divine intervention: a god helping and entering into personal relations with men, and that is something that natural human reason could not have suspected had God not revealed it. It is enough, then, that notwithstanding the lack of explicit and known statements, the divine light acting in souls should clarify this tradition for genuine, supernatural faith to be possible among pagans who have not wilfully rejected the light.

And if that was possible before Christ came, it is possible subsequently, for the sake of those who, not having sufficient knowledge of Christ, still await the salvation promised and already sent by God. As for those who call themselves atheists, it all depends upon whether they are really so or only apparently so. The latter type rejects what the word "God" means to him, but perhaps it is a caricature of the true God, a false god and an idol, which he thus rejects, while he accepts the reality of God without being able to give a name to it, by believing in some "Absolute", some "Good", to which man is subordinated. What we have just explained therefore remains possible in such a case. On the contrary, faith and grace are clearly impossible in the case of the real atheist, who rejects not only the name but the very reality of God, by denying that there is any Absolute, any Good, to which man owes submission.

We need not seek to probe further into the action of grace in the depths of souls. We cannot and must not judge our neighbour: that right belongs to God alone, but we know that in every human being in whom there subsists a minimum of freedom, and therefore the possibility of an interior motion of love towards God—even a criminal or a mental defective—or one whose mind has been deformed by a bad upbringing, even one whose intellect is erroneous, there is an interior action of the grace of God in the deepest centre of the soul which can call forth a response of love to the gift of a love that is infinite.

CONCLUSION

A "SPIRITUALITY OF GRACE"

The majority of our contemporaries are seeking the human and spiritual development of man by means of his natural spiritual faculties. They thus set before us a "spirituality" dependent upon man's own initiative and human effort, a "spirituality" made to the measure of our natural capacities, a "spirituality" in which man tends to surpass himself and rise rapidly towards God; and this tendency is to be found in all the seeking after heroism, ascesis, spiritual methods and techniques. Others, influenced by Marxism, seek the spiritual advance of man in his efforts to dominate nature, transform creation, in his dedication to temporal activities. They talk about "a spirituality of action", "a spirituality of labour", "a spirituality of dedication".

Unfortunately, many Catholics allow themselves to be misled by such tendencies, yet what is here in question is a matter of serious error, false religion and false mysticism, all of which is incompatible with the Christian faith. On the one hand, they fail to recognize, or reject contemptuously, the truth that since original sin man has been turned away from God and has fallen back upon himself. He stands in need of salvation or redemption if he is to be restored to his former state. On the other hand, they likewise fail to recognize that the true destiny of man, as God has revealed it, is a supernatural one, infinitely surpassing all our capacities or natural aspirations. No human effort, no ascesis, no technique or method, no dedication to action or labour, can enable man to emerge from his sinful condition, rise up to God, and make his way to his true spiritual destiny. A man is a Christian only when he has come to understand that it is not man who ascends to God, but God who comes down to give himself to us, and that from God comes all initiative.

The basis of all real Christian spirituality lies in realizing our true supernatural destiny, that of ourselves we can do nothing, that our supernatural destiny is a gift of God, that everything therein proceeds from the initiative of divine love. In other words, all true Christian spirituality is a spirituality of grace, a spirituality that is the flower and fruit of grace in us, a spirituality in which we are before God as beggars, who can only receive and who look for everything from his love. Christian spirituality rests wholly upon grace, it consists in opening our hearts to grace, letting grace take complete possession of us, transform us, sanctify us, deify us, as a little child abandons itself to its parents allowing itself to be dealt with as they wish.

Hence the only obstacle to grace is pride, self-will, independence, the determination to find everything in oneself. Christian spiritual life consists in recollecting ourselves within, there to find grace and live by it: to allow ourselves to be loved by God who gives himself to us. It means complete, loving surrender of ourselves to him who loves us. Whoever thinks he is anything of himself is condemned with the pharisee of the Gospel. Whoever believes that he is nothing, and acknowledges himself a sinner and incapable of anything good, but like the publican humbly begs God for mercy, will be saved.

That is why the Church has given us as a spiritual teacher St Teresa of Lisieux, whose whole spirituality is one of grace or, which comes to the same thing, of "spiritual childhood". It is the attitude of a very small child who does not consider itself capable of anything, but expects everything from its parents, and is ready to receive everything from them. Because God created us in order to impart to us his own divine life, and gives us the absolute and perfect joy which he is himself, we must be always with him, as little children in whom everything comes from him. Therefore, with the revelation of grace, which is God's declaration of his love towards men, we must ceaselessly repeat: "A man cannot see the kingdom of God without being born anew",[1] and "unless you become like little children again, you shall not enter into the kingdom of heaven",[2] that kingdom of which the gate is narrow because only he can pass through who is very small. It is to these "little ones" that the good tidings were proclaimed: *Peace to men who are loved by God.*

[1] John 3. 3.
[2] Matt. 18. 3.

SELECT BIBLIOGRAPHY

HENRY, A. M., O.P.: *Theology Library*, Volumes 1–4, Cork, Mercier Press and Chicago, Fides, 1956–8.

JOYCE, G. H., S.J.: *The Catholic Doctrine of Grace*, London, Burns Oates, 1920, and Westminster, Md, Newman Press, 1950.

MARMION, Dom Columba: *Christ the Life of the Soul*, London, Sands, and St Louis, Herder, 1922.

D'ARCY, M. C., S.J.: *The Nature of Belief*, London and New York, Sheed and Ward, 1931.

SCHEEBEN, Matthias J.: *Nature and Grace*, St Louis, Herder, 1954.

VONIER, Dom Anscar: *The Human Soul*, *Christianus*, *The Personality of Christ*, *The Spirit and the Bride*, all reprinted in *The Collected Works*, 3 Volumes, London, Burns Oates, and Westminster, Md, Newman Press, 1952–3.

SHEED, F. J.: *Theology and Sanity*, London and New York, Sheed and Ward, 1947.

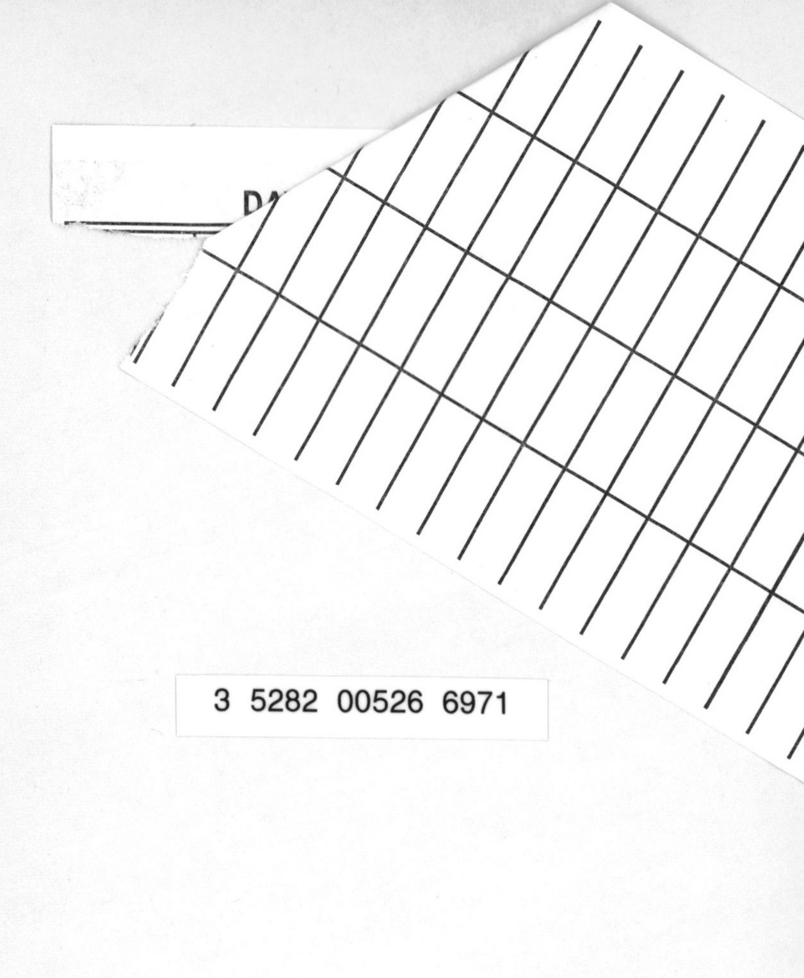
3 5282 00526 6971